Richmond Mayo-Smith

Emigration and Immigration

A Study in Social Science

Richmond Mayo-Smith

Emigration and Immigration
A Study in Social Science

ISBN/EAN: 9783742810670

Manufactured in Europe, USA, Canada, Australia, Japa

Cover: Foto ©ninafisch / pixelio.de

Manufactured and distributed by brebook publishing software (www.brebook.com)

Richmond Mayo-Smith

Emigration and Immigration

EMIGRATION AND IMMIGRATION

A STUDY IN SOCIAL SCIENCE

BY

RICHMOND MAYO-SMITH, A.M.

Professor of Political Economy and Social Science in Columbia College, Membre de l'Institut International de Statistique, Vice-President of the American Statistical Association, Etc.

NEW YORK
CHARLES SCRIBNER'S SONS
1898

COPYRIGHT, 1890,
BY CHARLES SCRIBNER'S SONS.

TYPOGRAPHY BY J. S. CUSHING & CO., BOSTON.
PRESSWORK BY BERWICK & SMITH, BOSTON.

CONTENTS.

CHAPTER I.

INTRODUCTION: THE NATURE OF THE QUESTION TO BE DISCUSSED AND OF THE PHENOMENA TO BE OBSERVED.

	PAGE
Social problems change from age to age	1
The fundamental political questions have reached a solution	1
While the economic and social-ethical are more prominent than ever.	2
The purpose and end of social organization	3
From this standpoint we must decide all social questions ✓	3
The importance of immigration is in its effect on civilization,	4
Characteristics of American civilization	5
Effect of immigration on our political institutions . . .	6
On our social morality	7
On our economic well-being and social traits	8
Difficulties of social science.	8
Immigration is a very complex phenomenon	9
Method of investigation in such a question as immigration .	10

CHAPTER II.

The History of Emigration.

	PAGE
Early migrations were either for conquest or colonization	12
Colonial expansion changed the whole aspect of the world	13
Emigration differs from colonization and is a modern movement	15
The statistics of emigration are not very satisfactory	15
The history of the movement, especially from Great Britain and Germany	17
Emigration from all European countries, 1887 and 1888	19
Effect of emigration on population	21
Comparison of emigration with the excess of births over deaths	23
It is not a remedy for the evils of over-population	24
Why European governments look with disfavor on voluntary emigration	27
Causes of emigration are mainly economic	30

CHAPTER III.

The History of Immigration.

Influence of immigration is more important than that of emigration	33
It is the life history of countries of the New World	33
In one sense all the inhabitants of the United States are immigrants or their descendants	35
Distinction between colonists and immigrants	35
Population during the colonial period	37
Very little immigration during the period from 1783 to 1820,	39

Contents.   vii

	PAGE
Since 1820 we have a statistical record of immigration	41
Causes of immigration in past years	43
Modern means of transportation make immigration easy	45
Influence of immigrants sending back for their friends	48
Sex, age, and occupation of immigrants	50

CHAPTER IV.

IMMIGRATION AND POPULATION.

The astonishing growth of the United States	53
Due to three causes: — (1) free land	56
(2) Railroads; and (3) immigration	57
How much of our present population is due to immigration	58
Its influence on the race or ethnic composition of our population	62
The negro and the foreigner	64
Immigrants according to nationality	67
Persons of foreign birth and of foreign parentage by nationality	68
The distribution of the foreigners	69
The foreign born flock to the cities	71
Certain forces tend to assimilate these foreign elements	72
(1) Economic prosperity; and (2) the exercise of political rights	73
(3) The dominance of the English speech	74
(4) Intermarriage of foreigners with natives and with each other	75
The theory that mixed races are the strongest needs correction	77

CHAPTER V.

THE POLITICAL EFFECTS OF IMMIGRATION.

Large proportion of adults gives the foreign born great voting power 79
Only in late years has this excited any jealousy or apprehension 81
Our liberal naturalization laws require merely formal tests . 82
Why not require evidence as to character and fitness? . . 84
Recent court decisions show a tendency that way . . . 85
Bad influence of the foreign vote when it votes in a body . 86
Our degraded municipal administration due to it 87
Outbreaks of anarchism and socialism due to foreigners . 88
These theories strange to American life 90
Unrestricted immigration is a severe strain on democratic institutions 91

CHAPTER VI

THE ECONOMIC GAIN BY IMMIGRATION.

Our material resources have been developed largely by immigration 93
Shown by the number of foreign born in different occupations 94
The economic gain by immigration consists (1) of the amount of money the immigrants bring 97
This is offset partly by remittances home 99
And what they bring is less than the average wealth here . 101
(2) The value of the immigrant as a man 102
Sometimes measured by the cost of bringing him up . . 104
Sometimes estimated as equal to the value of a slave . . 107

Contents.

	PAGE
True value is the excess of future wages over expenses (Dr. Farr)	109
But the immigrant is of use to us only if we can make him useful	113
Do we need any more immigrants?	113
Three-fourths of them are unskilled laborers (not even farmers)	114
Of whom we have already a great supply	117
Progress of civilization demands less of this kind of labor	119
And it tends to congest in large cities where it is not needed	120
There is already a host of the unemployed in this country	121
Karl Marx's theory of the industrial proletariat	121

CHAPTER VII.
COMPETITION WITH AMERICAN LABOR.

Must consider not only gain in wealth by immigration, but also the effect on American labor	123
(1) Direct competition by immigration of skilled laborers is not great	125
But the immigrants learn trades after their arrival	126
The displacement of American labor	127
Relation between free immigration and a protective tariff	128
(2) The importation of laborers under contract	129
(3) Competition with immigrants having a lower standard of living	131
The Italians, French Canadians, Poles, and Hungarians	132
The revival of the "sweating system"	136
This competition is unfair to our working classes	138
The old immobility of labor is broken down	139

Contents.

	PAGE
And the American laborer is subject to competition from the world	140
The true office of competition is to spur on producers	141
And it benefits all classes, including the laborers	142
Evils of increased cheapness due to degradation of labor	143
The French Canadians and the Scandinavians	144

CHAPTER VIII.

SOCIAL EFFECTS OF IMMIGRATION.

Other sides of civilization besides political freedom and economic prosperity	147
Difficulty of measuring the social effects of immigration	148
Natural to expect high rates of mortality, vice, crime, etc., among immigrants, because they belong to the lower classes	150
Large proportion of adults has the same effect	152
Our mortality and morbidity statistics are not satisfactory	153
The amount of insanity due to immigration	153
The blind, deaf and dumb, crippled, diseased, etc.	155
The prisoners and convicts of foreign origin	157
The paupers and homeless children	158
Immigration the prevailing cause of illiteracy in the United States	161
Influence of immigration on general social traits	166

CHAPTER IX.

ASSISTED EMIGRATION AND IMMIGRATION.

Emigration in former times viewed with dislike	168
Encouraged for the sake of the colonies	169

Contents.

	PAGE
Afterwards in order to get rid of paupers and criminals	169
Early cases of this sort in Switzerland	171
Emigration assisted by local authorities, by charitable societies, by friends, by steamship agents	172
The British government has assisted paupers to emigrate	173
Protest of the United States	174
The Tuke Committee	176
The emigrants not welcomed in Canada	178
The National Association for State-Directed Emigration	180
The opposition of the colonies to assisted emigration	184
Other societies that assist emigration	185
Emigration assisted by remittances and prepaid tickets	186
Abuses connected with prepaid tickets	188
Induced immigration from Italy	190
Assistance to immigrants from side of colonies and new countries	193
The British Emigrants' Information Office	196
Emigration is now largely under artificial stimulus	196
State-assisted emigration destined to fail of its purpose	198

CHAPTER X.

PROTECTING THE EMIGRANT: THE PASSENGERS' ACTS.

Practical freedom of a man to choose his domicile	201
The state still feels an interest in the emigrant	203
Its diplomatic and consular service looks out for him	204
Passengers' acts regulate his treatment at sea	205
Modern efforts to regulate emigration agencies	207
The new Swiss emigration law	210
Hardships endured by early immigrants to this country	215
The United States Passengers' Acts	216

xii   *Contents.*

	PAGE
The legislation of the state of New York	217
Scandalous treatment of immigrants on landing at New York	219
The New York Commissioners of Emigration	220
Castle Garden	221
The head-money tax declared unconstitutional	223
Present relation between the state commissioners and the federal government	224

CHAPTER XI.

CHINESE IMMIGRATION.

Prohibition of Chinese immigration by the United States and Australia	227
Early declaration that migration and expatriation are inalienable rights	228
The treaties of 1844 and 1858 with China	229
The Burlingame treaty of 1868	231
Chinese are promised the same treatment as subjects of the most favored nation	233
Beginning of the anti-Chinese agitation	235
The history of Chinese immigration into California	236
Californian legislation against the Chinese	238
The investigating committee of 1876	242
Evidence as to the moral and social condition of the Chinese,	243
The economic effects of Chinese immigration	244
The Chinese do not assimilate with our civilization	247
The question in Congress	250
The treaty of 1880 allows the United States to restrict further immigration	253
The acts of 1882 and 1884 and harsh enforcement of them,	255

Brutal treatment of Chinese in America 257
Negotiations for a prohibitory treaty; their failure . . . 259
The prohibitory act of 1888. 262
The Chinese question in the British colonies 263
True grounds for the exclusion of the Chinese 265

CHAPTER XII.

RESTRICTIONS ON IMMIGRATION.

The right of immigration is not perfect 266
States often exercise the right to expel aliens 267
Police regulations in regard to residence of strangers . . 268
The new French decree requiring the registration of foreigners 270
Alien beggars and vagabonds commonly sent back . . . 272
The legislation of the United States restricting pauper immigration 273
The act against the importation of contract labor . . . 276
The control of immigration a necessity 277
Absolute prohibition of immigration not desirable . . . 279
But the present laws should be strictly enforced 280
The plan of consular certificates 281

CHAPTER XIII.

THE QUESTION OF PRINCIPLE.

Freedom of migration from the standpoint of political science 284
All mediæval life denied any such freedom 285
Expansion of industry and commerce destroyed the old restrictions 287

French philosophy established the principles of freedom
  and equality 288
Enormous benefit of the doctrine of the brotherhood of
  man 289
Immigration is a privilege granted by the state 290
Sometimes held to be a duty to admit strangers 291
The principle not always applicable 292
The notion that America is an "asylum for the oppressed," 293
Error in reasoning from the past experience of a country . 294
This country no longer offers the advantages it once did . 295
The control of migration by positive law 295
Seen in the present tendency of legislation 296
The principles of international law in the case 297
Revival of the doctrine of permanent allegiance 299
The sovereignty of a state over its own territory 300
A state should take care of its own unfortunates 301
And this is the higher ideal of international comity and of
  humanity. 301

BIBLIOGRAPHY 303
INDEX 309

EMIGRATION AND IMMIGRATION.

CHAPTER I.

INTRODUCTION: THE NATURE OF THE QUESTION TO
BE DISCUSSED AND OF THE PHENOMENA
TO BE OBSERVED.

SOCIAL problems change from age to age. The position of a nation, its external history, its inner development, the new demands made upon it by the *Zeit-Geist*, — all these things cause first one set of questions to be presented and then another. The earliest problems forced on the peoples of Europe by the evolution of history were political. The German tribes, as they emerged from the primeval forest and overwhelmed Roman civilization, began the great work of establishing a state-form and defining the limitations of nationalities. The struggles of the eleventh century and the subsequent period of the Reformation determined the rival spheres of church and state. The absolute monarchy destroyed the feudal system as a political institution and developed powerful nations in the place of petty local principalities. The French revolution overthrew privileged classes and accentuated the right of the individual man to liberty and safety. Finally, the establishment of the representative system all over Europe has given to the community the opportunity to use legislative power for the good of the whole in distinction from that of a class. Thereby the fundamental problems of state-life have been solved, at any rate for the time being. Political questions are now matters of detail: the machinery of government is so to be organized as to carry out the will of the community. The legal and political rights of the individual members of the community have been determined and are no longer matter of dispute.

On the other hand, the general economic and social problems are more pressing than ever. The distribution of wealth and well-being, the relative opportunity for attaining the desirable positions and the desirable things of life, the chances of success, the duties of man to man and of social classes to each other, — all these questions are more prominent than ever. The individual is making demands for himself whose satisfaction requires the intervention of the community. He intones a cry of distress that is an impeachment of the social organization. He talks about his "rights" as if society were there simply to look out for him. It is the era of individualistic demands for socialistic action of the state;

but the socialistic scheme is no longer altruistic nor utopian, but highly personal and practical.

In this condition of things, it is highly interesting and important to determine exactly what the state can do for the individual, and what the individual may justly expect from the state. This is not merely the old question of the "interference" of the state, as the economists used to define all governmental action, even that of taxation; neither is it merely the question of determining the "sphere of state action," as the newer economists and political philosophers would phrase it. It is rather the investigation of the fundamental purpose of social organization and state life. Has society an ideal, towards which it is struggling and which it desires to reach? Are social traditions to be preserved and present institutions developed and expanded until they are fitted to contain that national life to which patriotism aspires? Have we ethical ideals which we should like to see approaching fulfilment, and whose fulfilment would satisfy us as an advance in civilization?

It is from this standpoint that we are to test and decide the social questions that present themselves at the present time. The demand which is made, — is it consistent with our ideal of social progress? The influence which is to be allowed or discouraged, — does it make for the social end? What is our duty to the poor? What is our obligation to the laboring classes when competition threatens to ruin them? Why should the state interfere to check the free action of industrial forces?

It is from this standpoint that the phenomena of emigration and immigration become of lively concern to the communities which they affect. It is not the migration of a few thousand or even million human beings from one part of the world to another, nor their good or bad fortune that is of interest to us. We are concerned with the effect of such a movement on the community at large and its growth in civilization. Immigration, for instance, means the constant infusion of new blood into the American commonwealth, and the question is: What effect will this new blood have upon the character of the community?

In order to answer this question it will be necessary to consider for a moment the characteristics of our civilization which give it strength and worth. We can then appreciate the influence immigration has had upon these characteristics, and estimate the final effect of its continuance on the present scale. It will be necessary to notice the influence of immigration on the growth of population, and to follow the ethnic changes which are being wrought thereby. Equally important is it to observe the effect of immigration on the economic condition of the laboring classes in this country, — whether it is made better or worse. In the same way it is advisable to study the influence of the new-comers on the ethical consciousness of the community, — whether there is a gain or a loss to us. In short, we must set up our standard of what we desire this nation to be, and then consider whether the policy we have hitherto pursued in regard to immigration is calculated to maintain that standard or to endanger it.

Edmund Burke once said: "To make us love our country, our country ought to be lovely." In order that we may take a pride in our nationality and be willing to make sacrifices for our country, it is necessary that it should satisfy in some measure our ideal of what a nation ought to be. If there is to be patriotism, it must be a matter of pride to say, *Americanus sum.*

What now are the characteristics of American state and social life which we desire to see preserved? Among the most obvious are the following : —

(1) The free political constitution and the ability to govern ourselves in the ordinary affairs of life, which we have inherited from England and so surprisingly developed in our own history;

(2) The social morality of the Puritan settlers of New England, which the spirit of equality and the absence of privileged classes have enabled us to maintain;

(3) The economic well-being of the mass of the community, which affords our working classes a degree of comfort distinguishing them sharply from the artisans and peasants of Europe;

(4) Certain social habits which are distinctively American or at least present in greater degree among our people than elsewhere in the world. Such are love of law and order, ready acquiescence in the will of the majority, a generally humane spirit displaying itself in respect for women and care for children and helpless persons, a willingness to help others, a sense of humor, a good nature and a kindly manner, a national patriotism and confidence in the future of the country.

All these are desirable traits; and as we look forward to the future of our commonwealth we should wish to see them preserved, and should deprecate influences tending to destroy the conditions under which they exist. Any such phenomenon as immigration, exerting wide and lasting influence, should be examined with great care to see what its effect on these things will be.

The continued addition to our electorate of hundreds of thousands of persons who have had no training in self-government, who have other and quite different traditions of state action,— will this not tend to weaken our political capacity and self-reliance? Will it not also affect the adjustment of our institutions to our people, — an adjustment which is so necessary if the institutions are to work successfully? If the new bearers of our political life have neither the aspirations which our ancestors cherished nor the experience which we have inherited, — will not the homogeneousness of our social organization be seriously imperilled? A free ballot which was safe in the hands of an intelligent and self-respecting democracy, is no longer safe in those of an ignorant and degraded proletariat.

A code of morality which depended for its life and strength on a religious system thoroughly believed in must be undermined when other systems of thought are suddenly introduced not furnishing the same basis. The commands of morality are absolute and must have the sanction of perfect faith in order to be effective. To destroy the credibility of the sanction, without putting anything in its place, must for the time being be destructive of ethical action. However narrow the religious system, and however much it may need expanding and liberalizing, the development should come from within and not through destructive forces working from without. German scepticism, for instance, may be a natural product of German life and may furnish its own basis for ethical rules of conduct; but if it is not also a natural development of American ideas, it must work as a foreign substance in the organism of our national life.

Economic well-being is a difficult thing for a nation to acquire, and once acquired is too precious to give up without a struggle. Once lost it may require generations to attain again, even if the economic conditions are favorable. The standard of living in this country should be jealously guarded, so that our working classes should not either consciously or unconsciously lose it. It may be lowered in either of two ways. Excessive immigration may overstock the labor market and reduce wages; or immigrants accustomed to fewer of the comforts of life may supplant the native workmen. In either case we have brought undue pressure to bear on the mass of the people and have forced them down to a lower level. We have substituted the lower for the higher, and preferred that which is inferior.

The change in social ideals wrought by the infiltration of peoples having different customs and habits of life can be detected only as these elements gradually become dominant and as we see the decay of habitudes which we had valued. We then exclaim against the degeneracy of the times, forgetting that we ourselves have admitted the elements which have superseded the old.

The problems of social science are very complex. The manifestations of social life are so interwoven that it is difficult to trace the connection between them. Even where one influence can be disentangled from others, it is almost impossible to measure its exact effect. The result may be neither direct nor immediate. It may manifest itself only through secondary phenomena or after the lapse of some years. It is impossible to reach exact conclusions, however sure we may be that the conclusions are certain. The very characteristics of a science, the exact classification and the power to predict results, may often be painfully lacking.

In no department of social science is this more true than in the entire range of questions pertaining to population. We readily perceive that one population differs from another, and we are able in a very general way to characterize the difference. We can often see that national traits are changing with the passage of time, and we can indicate in a general way the direction of the evolution. But to define the difference precisely, or to specify the exact cause of the change, is beyond our power.

So it is with immigration. It is a very complex phenomenon. The quantity of immigration varies from year to year. Still more does the proportionate quantity vary, *i.e.*, the number of immigrants compared with the number of the population receiving them. The quality of the immigration does not remain the same; and the conditions of industrial and social life, whereby a country is able or not able to assimilate the foreign material, are not easy to determine. Many of these things depend upon relations which cannot be measured and which can only, so to speak, be felt. We feel instinctively that such and such elements are incompatible with our social life, but we are not able to produce the technical proof. We are morally certain, but we cannot make the evidence scientifically complete. In a few years the new elements become inextricably intermingled with the old, and it is impossible to trace any national characteristic to either alone. There is constant reflex action, and the native modifies the foreign as much as the latter does the former. Finally, it may be only national prejudice that is struck by the change which, in the long run, may be desirable and not hurtful.

When we undertake, therefore, to investigate the good or disastrous effects of immigration on a large scale, only general results can be expected. As so often in social science, the method is somewhat indirect. Cause and effect cannot be precisely determined. It is only possible to say that such and such forces tend to produce such and such results. In the present study we must collect the facts and carefully observe the following points: We must measure the intensity of the immigration; for it is to be supposed that when it becomes very large, absolutely or relatively to the number of persons of native descent, some marked effects will follow.

We are to observe the quality of the immigration; for it is to be supposed that the more alien the immigrants to our blood and mode of life, the more difficult the process of assimilation will be, and the greater the friction and interruption to a simple and harmonious development. The character of the attractive force drawing the immigrants is of importance; for, obviously, where the force is an ignoble one the result will not be so desirable as where it is purifying or energizing. We must determine whether the difficulties of migration put in any way a test on the character of the immigrant, so that a process of natural selection is instituted whereby the desirable elements push through and the undesirable ones are left behind. Finally, we must study the indirect evidence of the influence of immigration in the statistics of the participation of the foreign born in vice, crime, illiteracy and other disastrous social phenomena. It is only by a combination of all these elements that we can reach a judgment of the effect of such a movement on the well-being of the community in which we are interested. It will be impossible to separate strictly the good from the bad, but we can attain results of sufficient precision to guide us in state action.

CHAPTER II.

THE HISTORY OF EMIGRATION.

EMIGRATION and immigration, as we understand them, are phenomena of modern life. Of course, from the beginning of human history there have been migrations of men. In early times these consisted of movements of whole tribes in a career of conquest and differed radically from emigration which is a movement of individuals. A second sort of migration began with the discovery of America and of the new route to India around the Cape of Good Hope and may be called colonization.[1] The newly discovered countries were utilized at first merely for the purpose of booty and afterwards for the establishment of trading posts or factories.

Considerable numbers of Europeans went out to these colonies as officials and soldiers, or as bankers, merchants and planters. The natives furnished the labor which was either slave or free,—generally the former,—and thus we have the peculiar colonial conditions as exhibited in the coffee-growing colonies of

---

[1] See Roscher and Jannasch, Kolonien, Kolonialpolitik und Auswanderung. 3d Ed. Leipzig, 1885. Leroy-Beaulieu, De la Colonisation chez les peuples modernes. 2d Ed., Paris, 1881.

the East Indies, the sugar-growing colonies of the West Indies, and on a large scale in the great imperial possession of India. The value of these colonies was almost entirely commercial. The planters received their capital and supplies from the home country and naturally disposed of their products and made their purchases there. The official posts furnished lucrative places for the younger sons of the nobility or the governing classes, but the colony was no real outlet for surplus population.

A second class of colonies differed radically from these. They were the agricultural colonies or plantations where people came for the purpose of settling and cultivating the soil. These persons expatriated themselves with the intention of making their permanent home in the new country. They did not intend merely to trade with the natives or to superintend servile labor, but to build up a community which should be self-supporting and which should after a while enjoy the same civilization as the mother country. At the same time they did not separate themselves from the parent, but continued under its political control and with the most friendly and loyal feelings towards it. They were still Englishmen, or Frenchmen, or Dutch just as they had been at home.

It is not too much to say that the colonial expansion of the seventeenth and the eighteenth century changed the whole aspect of the world. We can scarcely picture to ourselves the limitations of mediæval life confined within the bounds of Western Europe. It is difficult to conceive the narrow relations, the limited resources, the petty struggles of the nations of that day. The extension of colonies established the world commerce and brought the products of the whole earth to the inhabitants of Europe; it magnified the scale of things tenfold.[1]

Even when the colonies in America rebelled against England and Spain and established themselves as independent nations, the results were not lost. The trade still remained, and also the language, customs and habits of life. The civilization of the new world was simply a new European civilization and the expansion of Europe still went on. It is true that it was no longer an expansion of particular nations. The wanderers from Europe, if they went to the United States or to South America, gave up their home connection. But they still went principally to a country where either their language was spoken or the people were of a kindred race. The causes which had driven the original colonists from

---

[1] Roscher points out how colonization has changed the relative position of nationalities. It has made the English race and speech dominant in the world. The painful effort of the Germans to find unoccupied places for colonies so that Germany may become a "world-empire" is evidence of the same thing.

their home were often religious or political persecutions. Such refugees can still find a welcome in the United States where they have liberty of religion and protection against political punishment. In these cases, however, the movement is no longer a national but a private one. The state which sends out its citizens is no longer transplanting them to another part of its own dominion, but is giving them up to a foreign nation. The migrations of the nineteenth century are not colonization, but emigration.

This new movement is peculiar to the nineteenth century and has grown in intensity until it has become an important phenomenon of social life. It is worth our while to study carefully its progress, its causes and the effects which have followed in its train. It is not to be judged by the previous migratory efforts of the world, but should be considered on its own basis and with respect to its own influence on the civilization of modern Europe. Analogy of names should not confuse our perception of real differences in influence. Neither are we blindly to follow principles laid down at a time when the relations were of an entirely different kind.

The statistics of emigration are not very satisfactory. We have three sources of information. The first is the permits which formerly were universally required and are to-day in many states in order that a man may leave his country. The number of these permits never represents the real emigration because modern means of transportation are so extensive that it is easy to get beyond the frontier without them.

Then we have statistics of the departures from the principal ports. Those of Great Britain are the most complete in this respect because her frontier is entirely water. For Germany we have statistics of the departures by way of Hamburg, Bremen, Stettin and Antwerp, which represent the greater part of the German movement, but not the whole. Finally, we have the statistics of arrivals in new countries such as the United States, Australia, etc. By a combination of these last two bodies of figures (departures and arrivals) we can calculate approximately the strength of the migratory movement from year to year, and from each country.

These statistics do not reach back very far. The United States began to collect them in 1820. Most of the countries of Europe do not give us reliable statistics till a much later date. We know enough however to get a general picture of the movement from decade to decade and even from year to year. At the beginning of the century it was slight. Almost the only emigrants were from Great Britain and a few from Germany. The difficulties of travel were so great and the knowledge of new countries was so vague that very few persons in the more back-

The History of Emigration. 17

ward and less maritime countries had the courage to attempt the long and arduous journey.

From Great Britain the number of emigrants for the year 1815 was only 2,081. The next year it rose to 12,510, in 1817 to 20,634, in 1818 to 27,787 and in 1819 to 34,787. These were dark years in England and it is not surprising that some of the surplus population released from the war, in poverty and misery, should take refuge in the colonies and the United States. The number steadily decreased until 1824 when it was only 14,805. The commercial crisis of 1826 seems to have given a new impulse to the movement, and in 1832 the unusual number of 103,140 was reached. During the next years, down to 1845, the emigration averaged about 75,000 annually. In 1846 the Irish famine started a great movement, which continued until, in 1852, the number of emigrants was 368,764. Down to this time the statistics give us only the number of emigrants leaving the United Kingdom without distinguishing whether they are of British birth or not. From the year 1853 we have the two figures kept apart. The total number of emigrants of British and Irish birth that year was 278,129. Since that time the emigration from Great Britain has fluctuated from year to year, but we may say that every year between two and three hundred thousand British subjects are accustomed to leave their country in order to seek homes elsewhere. The greater part of this emigration has always been to the United States, but considerable streams have flowed to Canada and to Australia.[1]

German emigration presents very much the same development as British except that the large numbers come a little later. From 1819 to 1829 the German emigration is said to have been scarcely 5,000 persons per annum. From 1830 to 1843 it is estimated as only 22,000 per annum. In 1847 it rose to 110,434 and in 1854 to 251,931 from causes similar to those that had led to the increase in the British emigration.[2] Only once since then has it approached that figure.

Emigration from the other countries of Europe is a phenomenon of more recent date. As is well known, the French do not emigrate in large numbers. The Scandinavians have followed most closely the example of their kinsmen in Germany and England. The Swedish emigration was insignificant in numbers until 1867 when for the first time it amounted to nearly 10,000. In 1869 it rose to 39,064 and then declined, reviving however in 1879, and reaching a maximum of 50,178 in 1882. The Norwegian emigration goes back further than the Swedish, but has not grown so rapidly during recent years; it

[1] Complete statistics in the Italian Report on Emigration, 1886.
[2] Roscher and Jannasch, Kolonien, Kolonialpolitik und Auswanderung, s. 330. The figures include all emigrants from German ports.

The History of Emigration. 19

reached a maximum in 1882 of 30,214. The Italian emigration numbered nearly 20,000 in 1876, increased suddenly to 40,000 in 1879, and has since gone on increasing till in 1888 it was 195,993. This is the emigration to countries outside of Europe which the Italians call "permanent" emigration as distinct from "temporary" emigration (94,743 in 1888) to neighboring countries with the intention of returning.[1]

The present strength of the emigration movement may be seen by the following figures of emigration from the different countries of Europe during the years 1887 and 1888.

	1887.	1888.
Italy	127,748	195,993
Austria	20,156	24,819
Hungary	18,270	17,630
Germany	99,712	98,515
Great Britain and Ireland[2]	281,487	279,928
Denmark	8,801	8,659
Sweden	46,556	
Norway	20,741	
France	11,170	23,339
Belgium	3,834	7,794
Holland	5,018	

[1] Bulletin de l'Institut international de Statistique. Tome II. 2ème livraison, p. 25. Tome III. 2ème livraison, p. 95. Tome IV. p. 136. The figures for 1888 are not yet complete.

[2] England, 1887, 168,221; 1888, 170,822. Scotland, 1887, 34,365; 1888, 35,873. Ireland, 1887, 78,901; 1888, 73,233.

Switzerland	7,558	8,346
Russia	29,355	38,747
Spain	37,200	
Total	717,606	

It thus appears that in one year over 700,000 people from the different countries of Europe left them for the purpose of seeking homes elsewhere. The real number was probably greater than that, for the enumeration would often be incomplete. We know from the statistics of the United States, Canada, Australia and New Zealand, Argentine, Uruguay and Brazil that the immigration into those countries amounted to 1,116,000 in 1887, and there are many other countries that have some immigration. There is of course a backward current of immigration into Europe; but allowing for this, it is safe to say that in 1887 a million people left Europe with the intention of never returning. Many years the number has been greater.

It is not necessary to say that a movement on such a scale as this must have important consequences for the nations of Europe. It is a steady abstraction of a fraction of their population, whether for good or evil. It is not evenly distributed, but is much greater in some countries than in others. It cannot be measured solely by the absolute numbers, for some countries have a large population and can stand an emigration which would be ruinous to others. The quality of the emigration must also be taken into consideration, for the loss of persons from some classes in society is much easier to bear than that of others. We must therefore carry our analysis a little further. We shall do this very briefly, for the same facts will come out again in our consideration of the character of the immigration into this country.

There are two things to be considered in the question of emigration: one is the effect on population, and the other is the effect on the economic condition of the country. It is difficult to measure either with perfect accuracy.

Emigration is a direct drain on the population of a country, and this is to be measured by the proportion of the emigrants to the total number of inhabitants. Such figures we have in a very simple form. For instance, out of every 1,000 inhabitants of Italy in 1888 there emigrated 6.87; of France, 0.61; of Great Britain and Ireland, 7.46; of England and Wales, 5.97; of Scotland, 8.88; of Ireland, 15.06; of Germany, 2.10; of Switzerland, 2.85; of Sweden (1887), 9.86; of Norway (1887), 10.58; of Denmark, 4.01.[1] This gives us at once a vivid picture of the strength of the migratory tendency in the different countries of Europe without regard to the absolute numbers from each country.

[1] Bulletin de l'Institut, etc. IV. p. 190.

We can carry out a similar comparison for different parts of the same country; as for instance, the emigration from Germany as a whole during the year 1888 represented a proportion of only 2.10 per 1,000 of the population; but for Würtemberg it was 3.23; for Prussia it was 2.22, and for certain parts of Prussia it was, Pomerania, 4.81, and Posen, 7.24.[1] We can also study the strength of the migratory movement from year to year; as, for instance, we know that in Prussia emigration has been steadily working its way eastward from the Rhine provinces to the Baltic. In Ireland, the counties differ in the strength of this disposition to emigrate. In 1886 the average emigration of natives of Ireland was 12.2 to every 1,000 of the population; but the western counties were all above this average, and in the following order:—county Clare, 20.3; county Kerry, 20.2; Leitrim, 19.4; Galway, 16.1; and Sligo, 15.1. It can also be shown by statistics that while the migratory tendency increased in Ireland from 1878 to 1883, two and one-half fold, it increased in these western counties from three to seven fold during the same period.[2] It is evident that we have here an exact statistical method of measuring the strength of the emigration tendency in different countries and at different times.

---

[1] *Ibid.* p. 146.
[2] Emigration Statistics for Ireland, 1886.

The History of Emigration. 23

The effect on population can best be measured by comparing the figures of proportionate emigration with the figures of the increase of the population by excess of births over deaths. It is well known that, with one important exception, emigration does not seem to retard population, because it is precisely the countries having the largest emigration that have the largest birth-rate, so that the second makes up for the first. Thus in Germany in 1882, while the emigration was 4.25 per 1,000 inhabitants, the excess of births over deaths was 11.52 per 1,000. The loss by emigration was more than made up by the births. So also, in England and Wales, while the emigration was 6.17 per 1,000 of the inhabitants, the excess of births over deaths was 14.29 per 1,000. The great exception to this rule is Ireland, where in 1882 the emigration was 16.50 per 1,000 of the population, and the excess of births over deaths was only 6.66 per 1,000.[1] Emigration causes a constant decrease of the population in Ireland. In some of the provinces of Prussia in like manner there is an excess of emigration over the natural increase of the population.

Emigration does not threaten to depopulate the countries of Europe. Had there been no emigration during this century, it is not probable that the population of Europe would have been any

[1] Emigrazione Italiana, 1886.

greater than it is. The probabilities are all the other way. Europe has never grown so fast as during the present century. The commerce with the new world, the possibility of escaping thither, the supplies of food and raw commodities drawn thence have given a hopefulness and elasticity to European life such as it never had before. The place of the emigrants has been filled by new births, and more than filled. Even in Ireland, emigration has not succeeded in depopulating the country, for although in some counties like Clare and Kerry it is estimated that since 1851 emigration has carried off 72 per cent of the average population, those counties are still over-populated.

From the beginning of this century emigration has been looked to as a cure for the evils of over-population. Economists who held to the doctrine that wages depended upon the relation of capital to population, advocated it on the ground that it would prevent excessive competition in the labor market and thus raise the standard of living. These hopes have proved fallacious. As shown above, the growth of population is not at all impeded by such removals. The deficit is rapidly made up. Before the new standard of life is reached, the number has been regained, and the condition of the community is no better than it was. No such result could be attained except by the removal *en masse* of a very large number of persons. This could be done only by a government that would undertake the enormous expense of transporting the emigrants to a colony and settling them there so that they could earn their own living. No government has as yet been willing to undertake such a task. The English government has offered aid to the Irish to emigrate, but this aid has not been extensively made use of and has not in any sense been effective in diminishing the misery of the whole country. The condition of Ireland is little better now than it was forty years ago, notwithstanding the enormous emigration which has taken place of its own accord.

Emigration by itself is not a remedy for the evils of over-population or of a low condition of the mass of the people. It is important for us to remember this, for it is often assumed that by allowing free immigration into this country we are relieving the miseries of Europe, and helping to raise the people there to a higher standard of comfort and well-being. The abstraction of population must be accompanied by measures at home for bettering the condition of those classes which need elevation.

As emigration does not relieve over-population in general neither does it relieve congestion of population in particular districts, nor over-crowding of land in particular sections. In Prussia, the emigration comes now from the poorly settled districts of the

East, and not from the densely settled Rhine provinces. The difficulty is that emigration is controlled by other motives which may have absolutely no connection with the desirability of removing certain elements of the population or relieving the social pressure at certain points. It is often the poor and degraded who have not the courage nor the means to emigrate, and who remain in a life constantly growing harder and more hopeless. The mere accident of good transportation facilities often has more influence in determining the stream of emigration than do any social causes whatsoever.

It can scarcely be expected that a mere blind movement following a variety of motives shall of itself, without leadership, work out good social results. There is absolutely nothing in the movement of free emigration which could lead us to expect that its results would invariably, or even on the whole, be for the good of the community which the emigrants leave. Blind forces must produce chance results, and the probability is that the results will not be what were expected. Emigration does not bring about a decrease of population; neither does it relieve congestion of population, nor remove the burden of poverty and low-living which has been caused by an excess of population. These results are mostly negative. If we turn to the economic effects of emigration things appear in a more positive light.

The History of Emigration. 27

It is a curious fact that most of the governments of Europe are opposed to emigration in its present form. This opposition is partly because it represents, in many cases, an evasion of the universal military duty. During the years 1872 and 1873, which were good years for the working classes of Germany, there were not less than 10,000 processes annually for evasion of military duty by emigration.[1] The military authorities naturally look with disfavor upon this desertion of the fatherland at a time when it calls upon its youths to serve it. In some cases the large emigration of agricultural laborers has given rise to a scarcity of labor and excited the fears of the landlords and also of those who look upon the farming class as the conservative foundation of the whole national life. This is the case in Italy at the present time, and has been the case in Sweden and Norway, where the population is scanty and where the emigration if it continues threatens to leave a portion of the country without inhabitants.

If we look at the matter from the standpoint of the whole nation, we can readily perceive the reason for the sceptical attitude of the European communities towards free and voluntary emigration. When emigration is brought about by the free action of a man's own mind, without extraneous aids or influ-

---
[1] Schönberg, Handbuch der Politischen Oekonomie. 2 Aufl. II. 965.

ences, it is naturally the men who have intelligence, some financial resources, energy and ambition that emigrate. It requires all these to break loose from the ties of kindred, of neighborhood and of country, and to start out on a long and difficult journey. Voluntary emigration, as was pointed out by Thorold Rogers some years ago,[1] would naturally expatriate the cream of the working classes. This position is partly proven by statistics, by which, indeed, we cannot measure a man's character, but which give us some particulars in regard to age and sex that are useful indices of the strength and capacity of the emigrant. It is well known that a majority of the emigrants, generally sixty per cent, are males. This in itself is an indication of economic strength, for men are stronger and more self-reliant than women. This excess of males is due to the large number of unmarried men who migrate. An additional fact in this connection is that the majority of the emigrants are in the most vigorous ages of manhood and womanhood. Of the German emigrants, for instance, over sixty per cent are between the ages of fifteen and forty, although only thirty per cent of the population are between those ages.[2] Not only do the emigrants come from the best ages, but the drain on

---

[1] Manual of Political Economy. 3d ed., 1876.
[2] Rümelin, in Schönberg, Handbuch, etc. II. S. 916.

the adult men of the country is twice as great as on any other class.

It is true that emigration does not decrease population, because the places are taken by new births, but this is not a paying process for Germany. She has the expense of bringing up her children to manhood, and then loses the benefit of their labor and commences the nursing process again. She is left with an abnormal proportion of children, of old people and of the weak and disabled; while the new country is provided with able-bodied adult laborers at her expense. The only offset to this would be a compulsory emigration by which she could get rid of the weak and the infirm, — those who are a burden to the community. We therefore find the authorities of Europe generally opposed to voluntary emigration, while in some cases engaged in or encouraging secretly the emigration of the poor and the vicious. The economic and social gain or loss by emigration is determined more by the character of the emigrants than by their number. It is not an easy thing to say how far it is a benefit and how far an injury to any country at the present time. There are very few nations that would be willing to encourage it on any great scale and most of them prefer to have their people stay at home.

Of course there are circumstances in which the chance to leave one's country is in every sense a gain, both to the emigrant and to the country itself. The leaders of a party that has been defeated in a civil war find it more congenial to live in a new country than to stay under the rule of their opponents, and it is for the peace of the country that these restless spirits are removed. So in case of the decline of a national industry, it is a gain that the workmen can leave the neighborhood where there is no longer employment for them. Those who have been persecuted for their religion have often found safety in expatriating themselves. Even the vicious may occasionally use the new opportunity to begin a more creditable career.

With the causes of this immense migratory movement of the nineteenth century it will be better to deal further on under the study of immigration, when we shall attempt to analyze them more closely in order to study the worth of the immigrant. It is sufficient to say here that religious and political motives have sunk into insignificance. There was a time when men were compelled to leave their country in order to enjoy religious freedom, and that movement has given birth to some of the most solid and progressive colonial communities. But the growth of religious tolerance has abrogated that necessity; the only exception is the persecution of the Jews in Russia, and this seems to have as much of a social as of a religious side to it.

It is also true that down to this century men emigrated in order to escape political tyranny. Even after the insurrections and revolutions of 1848 political refugees fled to the United States. This occasionally happens in the case of nihilists and socialists at the present time. So also after Prussia incorporated the kingdom of Hanover, and after the German empire took possession of Alsace and Lorraine, many of the old inhabitants migrated rather than submit to the new régime; but such movements are also insignificant.

The main cause of emigration at the present time may be correctly described as economic. It is the desire to escape some economic pressure or to attain a better economic condition. The occasions for the working of the cause may be different, and the result may be fortunate or disastrous, but the cause is neither religious nor political but economic. This is seen when one studies the variations in the flow of emigration from one year to another. Whenever famine or hard times occur in the countries of Europe, there is an immediate increase in the flow of emigration. Whenever there is distress in the countries of the new world, there is a decrease in the volume of immigration. The causes are sure to be followed by the effects, although it may take some time for the cause to be fully felt and acted upon. Other influences may modify this primary one in a great variety of ways. The temptation to escape military duty is always present. An impending war in Europe might give a sudden stimulus to the movement, or a war in the United States might greatly retard or almost entirely check it.[1] The establishment of a new steamship line or the sudden reduction of the rates of fare has sometimes increased the emigration from a particular country or locality. The activity of steamship agents is an abnormal influence which has greater or less weight. Especially, the knowledge of the new country and the solicitations of relatives and friends who have already settled there are powerful inducements which work with more or less disregard of economic conditions. All these are minor variations but the general influence may still be said to be the desire to better one's economic condition.[2]

---

[1] See statistics of immigration in next chapter.

[2] Roscher (Kolonien, etc., S. 35) points out that one great inducement to colonization has been that, however hard the colonists may have to labor, the children will rise to a better position than they could ever have attained at home. Many of the pioneers in our Western states were actuated by the same motive. See Hugh McCulloch's experience in Indiana, Men and Measures of Half a Century.

CHAPTER III.

THE HISTORY OF IMMIGRATION.

IN many respects the history of immigration is much more interesting than that of emigration. The latter may have some effect in diminishing the population or the material resources of a country, although, as we have seen in the previous chapter, even such effects are not felt perceptibly in states having a vigorous life. At the worst it becomes one of the factors in the decline of those states which are losing their position among the nations of the world.

Immigration, on the other hand, is the life history of the countries of the new world. Through it we trace the beginning of that process by which the civilization of Europe has spread over the whole face of the globe. It is in itself the history of the new world. Still further, immigration directly increases population in the later stages of the history of these countries, — an increase that is independent of the relation of births and deaths and that has the most important influence in determining the position of the country among the other powers of the world.

The quality of the immigration also has important influence on the civilization of the new country. The ethnic constitution may undergo the most decided change by the addition of elements differing from the original population. The immigrants may be of different race or nationality, with different language, customs, or habits of thought from the people of the country that receives them. They may have been accustomed to different political institutions and not be able to adjust themselves readily to the political life of the new country. Economically, they may have been accustomed to a lower standard of living, and thus introduce a distressing competition in the labor market. Socially, they may represent an abnormal proportion of the classes that contribute to the pauperism, the crime and the vice of the community, and thus add to the burden of private and public charity. Whenever immigration assumes large proportions these questions are sure, sooner or later, to become very important.

It is only in recent times that these problems of immigration have presented a serious aspect. Of course wherever there is emigration there is a corresponding immigration, but the chief interest of the whole movement has hitherto been supposed to be to the country of emigration, and the question has been viewed entirely from that standpoint. All through the middle ages there was little immigra-

The History of Immigration. 35

tion in the real meaning of the word, for neither conquest nor commercial colonization can be said to have any immigration side to them. The stranger was generally looked upon with disfavor, where he was not absolutely excluded. There are instances where foreigners were admitted and even urged to come; as Edward III imported Flemish weavers into England in order to establish the cloth industry, and Colbert introduced Venetian glass-makers and Swedish iron-workers into France; but these are isolated examples and not of importance. It is needless to say that the introduction of Scotch and English into Ireland had the characteristics of a conquest rather than of immigration.

The history of immigration into the United States, to which we shall now confine ourselves, may be briefly traced as follows:—

In one sense all the inhabitants of the United States are immigrants or the descendants of immigrants. The only exception would be the few descendants of the aborigines, who still exist, but in a position of insignificance and utter inferiority. There is, however, a great difference between those who came to this country when it was an unclaimed wilderness, and by their toil and sacrifices established a great commonwealth, and those who simply migrate into a country where state, laws and customs are already fixed. The first are colonists; the second are merely immigrants. (To the first belongs the glory of having established the state and given to the new country its institutions, laws, customs and language. They are, in a sense, the founders and proprietors of the new state, and they have a right to guard its institutions from alien influences, if these should threaten danger to their integrity.) The second, the immigrants who have not shared the dangers of the period of settlement, occupy a subordinate position. They are not there through any merit of their own, but by consent and upon invitation of the original colonists. It is true that they may have aided in the material development of the country and in that respect have been of very great service, but they are still merely immigrants; they are not the founders of the state.

In the history of any new country it is not easy to draw the line between colonists and immigrants. In other words it is not easy to say exactly when the process of colonization is complete. In the case of the United States a convenient date is furnished by the conclusion of the war of independence against Great Britain. Down to 1783 may be termed the period of colonization. At that time the state was established, and any further additions to the population had little influence in changing its form or the language and customs of the people. Since 1783, the growth of population in the United States has been due to natural increase and to immigration. This period we can conveniently, although somewhat arbitrarily, divide into two. Our statistics of immigration begin in 1820. From 1783 to 1820 there seems to have been little immigration, so that we may call that the period of natural increase; and from 1820 to the present day we may call the period of immigration.

Our knowledge of the growth of population during the colonial period is extremely meagre. No accurate records were kept of new comers or of births and deaths. The data lie scattered through a great many books, tax lists, voters' lists, military levies, etc., and it is only by careful comparison of these and a knowledge of the laws of population that we can arrive at any conclusion. The latest estimates of this character are those made by Prof. F. B. Dexter and presented to the American Antiquarian Society at a recent meeting. The conclusions of this careful paper are summarized as follows:—

"In the first third of a century, or by 1640, when Parliament gained the ascendancy in England, British America contained a little over 25,000 whites,—60 per cent of them in New England, and the most of the remainder in Virginia. At the restoration of the monarchy in 1660, the total was about 80,000, the greatest gain being in the most loyal divisions, Virginia and Maryland, which now comprehended one-half the whole. At the next epoch, the Protestant Revolution of 1689, Mr. Bancroft concludes that our numbers were not much beyond 200,000, and the figures I have presented give about 206,000; in this increase one large factor was due to the Middle Colonies, which now for the first time assumed importance, numbering already nearly one-half as many as New England.

"A round half million appears to have been reached about 1721, with the Middle Colonies showing again the largest percentage of growth, and New England the least. A million followed in twenty-two years more, or 1743, this figure being doubled in turn twenty-four years later, or in 1767, — the latter reduplication being delayed a little, doubtless by the effect of intervening wars.

"In the Congress of 1774 the colonists ventured for the first time on a guess at their own strength, their estimate being a little over three millions; but the true number cannot have been much more than two millions and a half, and this in turn was double the figure reached about twenty-three years before, which period is the usual time of doubling shown by our later censuses down to the date of the civil war.

"These results differ slightly from those approved by Mr. Bancroft in his last edition, who exceeds my estimates from 1750 to 1770 by amounts varying from 50,000 to 100,000, or from 4 to 5 per cent of the totals."

(Note.) "My own figures are, for 1750, 1,207,000; for 1760, 1,610,000; for 1770, 2,205,000; for 1775, 2,580,000; for 1780, 2,780,000. The published figures of the census of 1790 (3,929,214) do not include Vermont or the territory northwest of the Ohio, which would bring the total above 4,000,000."[1]

The part played in this increase of population by colonization from the old world and by the natural

[1] Estimates of Population in the American Colonies, by Franklin Bowditch Dexter, Worcester, 1887.

increase of the original settlers is absolutely unknown. Considering the difficulties of getting to America and the dangers to be encountered there, it is probable that after the first settlement the increase was mainly natural, supplemented by an intermittent flow of new comers. The dangers of the frontier life were very considerable; but on the other hand there was no restraint on the increase of population due to the difficulty of providing careers for the children, so that a man could have as large a family as he chose. It is not improbable that the doubling period of twenty-three years represents the normal excess of births over deaths. Immigrants were naturally welcome, for there was always a demand for labor and a place for every able-bodied man.

For the period from 1783 to 1820 we know the actual number of the population at the censuses of 1790, 1800, 1810 and 1820. But during this period we have no statistics of immigration, so that we cannot tell how much of the growth was due to the natural increase of the people and how much to immigration. The increment — about thirty-five per cent during each decade — was large, but no larger than we should expect from the natural increase of population in a new country where there were few restraints. Everything was still in favor of early marriages and large families. On the other hand the period was not one that encouraged immigration. The colonies were not rich except in the necessaries of life; their political future was uncertain; their commerce and finances were in a state of confusion; and there could have been but little inducement to Europeans to undertake the difficult and dangerous voyage. During a great portion of the time the new republic was on an unfriendly and even hostile footing with the mother country, and commercial intercourse was often cut off by embargoes and wars. In accordance with this condition of things the notices that we find of actual arrivals of immigrants are scattering, and indicate an uncertain and sporadic movement. These notices have been collected by various writers who have attempted to calculate from them the total immigration during the period.[1] It is utterly impossible, however, to arrive at any conclusion, because the imformation is so meagre. The estimate that is commonly accepted, and the one that is published by the bureau of statistics, is that the number for the whole period was about 250,000.

The real history of immigration into the United States begins with 1820. Since that time the collectors of customs at the seaports in the United

---

[1] See Seybert, Statistical Annals of the United States, 1818; Chickering, Immigration into the United States, 1848; Tenth Census of the United States, vol. 1, p. 457.

States have been obliged to make a record of all passengers arriving by sea from foreign countries, also the age, sex and occupation of such passengers and the country to which they severally belong.

The statistics taken under this act are probably pretty accurate. In early years there may have been omissions, and there is a considerable over-land immigration much of which escapes enumeration, and which in fact since 1885 has been omitted entirely from the returns. Down to 1855 no distinction was made between aliens who were simply travellers and intended to return, and the *bona fide* immigrants who came to stay.

The tide of immigration has swollen enormously during the seventy years covered by this record. During the "twenties" the immigration was small, only ten or twelve thousand coming over annually, increasing to twenty thousand in 1826 and 1827, owing probably to the commercial depression in England. In the "thirties" it grew steadily, decreasing in the years 1836 and 1837, on account of the depression of trade in this country. The number first reached one hundred thousand in 1842, but sank the following year, showing that the normal figure at that time was somewhat less. In 1846 began the first of those great movements due to crises in the old world which have occurred frequently since and whose reflex action tends to keep the tide permanently strong. The combination of bad times in Germany and the famine in Ireland made the enormous maximum (427,833) in 1854. This number was not reached again until after the civil war. During that period, the conditions, especially the facilities for transportation, changed materially. Instead of sailing vessels, steamships came into general use. The voyage was shorter, the rates of fare were lower, and the efforts of transportation companies to obtain passengers much more persistent and wide-spread. The Western states were welcoming the immigrants and establishing immigration bureaux for the purpose of aiding foreigners to come and settle with them. Knowledge of the new countries was spreading, a great many persons had friends already here, and these friends were trying to induce them to come. The civil war had terminated in favor of free labor, and the enormous development of railroads had opened up a great territory to colonization and settlement.

The result of all this was the renewal of immigration immediately after the civil war. The years from 1867 to 1872 were years of immense business activity in the United States. Much of this activity was speculative and brought about by an inflated paper currency, but it gave employment to labor. So immigration went on and on until in 1872 it reached the figure of 437,750. Then the commercial depression stopped the flow for several years. With the apparent return of prosperity in 1879 and 1880, immigration commenced again, until in 1882 it reached the enormous number of 730,000. Since then it has gone down only to revive again, until at the present time the number is over half a million annually.[1]

The course of immigration into the United States may be pictured as a succession of waves. There is always a flood and an ebb, but the succeeding tide is, as a rule, higher than the preceding one. The movement increases although it does not do so by regular gradations, and there is no sign that we have reached the end of it, or even the end of the increase.

Immigration to this country is of course mainly from Europe, especially since we have absolutely prohibited the coming of the Chinese. The countries that contribute most largely to the number are Ireland and Germany. During the last few years a marked change has occurred, the proportion of Irish immigrants having fallen off and that of the German having increased. In recent years the Scandinavian immigration has steadily grown, as has also the Italian.

The causes of this enormous immigration have al-

[1] 1887 = 516,933; 1888 = 525,019; 1889 will probably show a decrease.

ready been partly indicated. Since 1820 over fifteen million persons have come to the United States and more than one-half of these have come since 1870. No cause that works merely on the disposition or the sentiments can account for such a movement. Some part has been due to political discontent, but that is no longer a determining influence. Political discontent is not so wide-spread in Europe to-day as it was in 1848. The socialists do not look upon the American republic as any nearer their ideal than the monarchies of Europe, and they find no better treatment here than at home. Again it is no potato famine now as it was in 1846. It is true that in the history of immigration we can trace the effect of economic distress in Europe in increasing emigration, and of economic distress in the United States in decreasing immigration. The great Irish emigration of 1846 and the great German emigration of 1853 were undoubtedly due to famine in the old countries. So also immigration to this country was decreased by the commercial disasters of 1836-37, by the civil war of 1861-64 and by the commercial depression of 1873. But absolute famine is not so frequent in Ireland as it once was, and mere hard times extend over the world and are commonly felt as keenly and at the same time in the United States as in Europe. Doubtless the immigrant does expect to better his economic condition by the migration, but it is not the direct pressure of want or the definite knowledge of how he will gain that leads him to change his domicile. The whole movement is more economic than political, but there are certain minor influences which are the immediate cause of the increase of immigration in recent years. These are as follows : —

The improved means of transportation at the present time make it very easy for persons to change their domicile. In former days the journey was long, difficult and expensive. The emigrant, if he lived in an inland town, had to reach the coast, and there await the sailing of some vessel. Then he was crowded into a small sailing ship, miserably fed, liable to sickness and disease, obliged to live in that way weeks and perhaps months, subject to the brutality of the captain and crew of an ordinary merchantman, and he was fortunate if he reached the other side not permanently enfeebled by some disease. Landing in the United States he had a long and expensive journey still before him if he wished to settle in one of the newer states.

Now all this is changed. The intending emigrant buys a ticket in his native village, the railroad transports him quickly and comfortably to the port where steamers leave regularly two and three times a week. The voyage lasts but eight or ten days. The owners of the vessel are obliged by law to provide him with comfortable quarters, — so and so many feet of space for each passenger, — with sufficient food, of good quality and well-cooked, and medical attendance. When he lands he can buy a railroad ticket to his point of destination and in a few hours find himself there. Steamships sail from every prominent port in Europe many times a week. For instance, in 1887, there were running to the port of New York alone steamers that made 259 trips from Liverpool and Queenstown, 265 from Bremen, Hamburg and Havre, 96 from Glasgow, 15 from London, 106 from Antwerp and Rotterdam, and 144 from other ports of Europe.[1] Some of these ships carry from a thousand to fifteen hundred steerage passengers.

Of course a regular transportation business on such a scale as this cannot be maintained except by a very extensive organization for the purpose of securing passengers. The Inman Steamship Company has thirty-five hundred agents in Europe, and an equal number in this country selling prepaid tickets to be sent to friends and relatives of persons already here in order to provide them with passage. In the little country of Switzerland, with one-half the population and one-third the area of the state of New York, there were, in 1885, four hundred licensed emigration agents. The object of these men is to

[1] Report of the Emigration Commissioners of the State of New York, 1888.

sell tickets and get their commission. They picture the advantages of America in glowing terms to the peasants and artisans and to any that are discontented with their lot. The young and ambitious, or the young and reckless, lend a willing ear; and even the married men go, expecting in a short time to earn easily sufficient to send for wife and children. In many cases they mortgage or sell the little farm or vineyard, which is their sole support, for the purpose of raising the money. In other cases the agent loans them the sum necessary, and they repay him with their first earnings on the other side.

Competition brings down the rate of fare. These great steamships must be filled, and filled at the time they sail. It is better to take people for something just above the bare cost of feeding them rather than to have the ship go empty. At one time, says a German official document, steerage passengers were carried from Hamburg to New York by way of England for the sum of seven dollars. During the steamship war of 1885 steerage rates were reduced to twelve and even ten dollars. In 1888 emigrants were carried from New York to Chicago for five dollars.[1] The moment a man is discontented the alluring prospect is held out to him, that by paying a small sum he can reach a country where everything will be better. The low rate of fare offers a great temp-

[1] Testimony before Ford Committee, pp. 5, 415.

tation to charitable societies and poor-relief guardians to get rid of the burden of paupers and persons unable to support themselves, by buying them a ticket to America, in the expectation that they will never be heard from again.

Another thing that has greatly increased the tide of immigration, and that keeps it large notwithstanding adverse influences, is the constant communication between those already here and the friends they have left behind. There is a steady flow of letters to the old country. The immigrants who have prospered here depict their success in the most glowing terms to old friends and acquaintances. In many cases they exaggerate, as is natural, determined to vindicate their own wisdom. Occasionally they revisit the old home in order to display their wealth and dilate on the advantages they have reaped. One such letter passed from hand to hand in a little village, or one visit of such a magnate, is more efficacious in sowing the seed of discontent and restlessness than many steamship agents. One after another is seized with the desire to try his luck, and the influence is continued from year to year and only waits for the fitting occasion to bear fruit. Again, many of these letters carry with them money or a prepaid ticket in order that the parent or the wife or the relative may follow in the steps of those who have made the first venture. Millions of dollars are sent back every year for the purpose of aiding friends to come over.

The result of all this is that emigration is no longer going among strangers. Almost every one has a relative, or a friend, or at least an acquaintance in the new country to whom he can look for aid and counsel on first arriving. To a man of almost any nationality this country is like a colony of the mother land. Here he finds countrymen, newspapers in his own language, people who are able to understand him, home customs, etc. It is no longer emigration in the sense of expatriation, but simply migration in the sense of moving from one part of the country to another. It no longer requires a violent wrench to detach a man from his domicile and transplant him to a new home; he does not leave after long deliberation, and only under the stress of absolute want or persecution; the slightest occasion is sufficient to persuade him to undertake an adventure which in former times would have been considered the most important event of his life. The same disposition to wander and to try one's fortune under new conditions, which is characteristic of our own people in their migrations from the East to the West, is being acquired by the peoples of Europe in this international movement.

Our statistics of immigration carry us one step further in the way of giving us a description of the immigrants as to sex, age and occupation. It is well known that a majority of the immigrants are males, generally about sixty per cent. The proportion varies, however, in an interesting way among different nationalities. The Irish show a very large proportion of females, owing doubtless to the large immigration of unmarried girls as domestic servants. Next in this respect come the immigrants from Nova Scotia and from Prince Edward Island, among whom there is often an excess of females. These girls find employment in New England as domestic servants and in the factories. Germany shows a greater proportion of females than any country of Europe except Ireland. This is due also to the employment of German girls as domestic servants, and points to another interesting fact, viz., that as the custom of emigration continues whole families are apt to go together. When a movement of emigration commences it consists mainly of unmarried men. They can best make their way alone in the new world. A few married men may come out alone and afterwards if they prosper they send for their families. Thus at the present time the Italians, the Hungarians and the Poles show a comparatively small percentage of females. The immigration of these nationalities is at the present time of the lowest kind of unskilled labor, and they have not the money to bring their families with them. So it has been noticed in the recent German statistics that the number of households emigrating tends to increase.

It is also well known that the immigrants are largely in the productive ages of manhood and womanhood. The figures for 1887 were as follows:

Under 15 years of age	94,278 or 17.18 per cent.
15 and under 40 years of age . . .	345,575 or 70.51 per cent.
40 years of age and upward . . .	50,256 or 12.31 per cent.

The proportions differ somewhat according to nationality. Germany shows an extraordinarily large number of children, due doubtless to the immigration by families noticed above. Ireland shows a large number in the period from fifteen to forty, and a correspondingly small number of children and persons above the age of forty. The apparent tendency in Ireland is for the youths of both sexes to emigrate before marriage.

These immigrants are mostly from the lower classes, the unskilled laborers, of Europe. Of all those who return an occupation, three-fourths are unskilled. We shall deal with these figures more in detail when we come to consider the economic effect of immigration.

We have now outlined this great movement of immigration as it has continued its course during the last seventy years and as it appears to-day. It remains for us to consider it more carefully and to attempt to define the effect it has had on the people and the institutions of the United States. Such effect cannot have been insignificant. It may have been for good or it may have been for evil. At any rate it is worth our while to follow out this great social movement in its details.

CHAPTER IV.

IMMIGRATION AND POPULATION.

NOTHING is more astonishing in the history of the United States than the rapidity with which its territory has been populated. The task that lay before the original settlers was immense. There was in front of them to be subdued a wilderness three thousand miles wide, covered with primeval forests, unbroken by roads and even unexplored. The colonist could have maintained his equanimity in the presence of this task only by ignoring it and contenting himself with an open frontier subject to Indian invasions as one of the ordinary conditions of existence. His life was a sort of constant picket duty, without relief or furlough, and practically without truce. But although the original settler did not trouble himself with the problem of how the whole continent was to be filled up and added to the realm of civilization, and although he probably had very vague notions as to when this result would be consummated, yet the spirit of history was busy with the task and brought it to a conclusion much sooner than could have been deemed possible. At first, as we have seen, the progress was extremely slow. The active force was only the original body of colonists, few in number and armed with the hand implements of the seventeenth century, — and not the best of these. The principal addition to this labor force came from the natural increase of the population, *i.e.* the excess of births over deaths. This excess was very considerable, although the mortality must have been large during the first few years of the settlement. But although the rate of increase was perhaps the largest of which we have any historic example, yet the basis for the increase was so insignificant that the absolute numbers remained small. At the close of the revolution there were less than three million men in the thirteen colonies. At the first census of the United States there were about four million.

We must picture to ourselves the population of the United States in 1790 as stretching along the coast from Maine to Georgia in a narrow belt. The depth, so to speak, of the inhabited area was scarcely two hundred and fifty miles at its deepest parts, and that was only where navigable rivers allowed settlers to ascend them and still keep up communication with the coast. The great mass of the people were on the seaboard or in its immediate neighborhood. The so-called cities were small and insignificant. The population was mainly agricultural, only three per cent living in towns of eight thousand inhabitants and over. It seemed as if the future republic might very probably be confined to this narrow strip along the seaboard. The Mississippi valley was still only half-acquired, and the occupation even of the Northwest Territory was hindered by the hostile attitude of the Indians incited by British agents. The means of communication were poor, and even if the western country were to be settled it would be difficult to hold it in political and social connection with the eastern coast. And if these difficulties were successfully surmounted, it must be a long time before the natural increase of population would create that density which is necessary in order that a nation shall enjoy the strength and prestige of high civilization.

During the first century of our national life all this has been changed. The whole continent stretching from ocean to ocean has been brought under the control of man. Our population has reached sixty or sixty-five millions, — equal to that of any first-class power in the world. Great commonwealths have sprung up in the Mississippi valley and on the Pacific slope. Distant sections have been brought into harmonious relations, and the different parts of the present community are more firmly united and feel more like the parts of one whole than did the colonies of a hundred years ago.

Three factors have been instrumental in bringing this about. They are the acquisition of territory, the building of railroads, and the immigration of people from Europe.

It is scarcely possible to exaggerate the influence of the plentiful supply of land on the social history of this country. It has permitted and encouraged the rapid increase of population, which, instead of growing denser, has spent itself in taking up new territory. Thus from 1820 to 1830 the population increased 32.51 per cent, but the settled area increased during the same period 24.4 per cent, so that the density of population in the settled area increased only 1.4 individuals to the square mile. From 1830 to 1840 population increased 32.52 per cent, settled area 27.6 per cent, and density only 0.8 individuals to the square mile. Even after 1840, when the immigration began to affect population so that it increased over thirty-five per cent in each of the decades following, the settled area increased nearly twenty-two per cent in each decade so that the density only increased from 21.1 persons to the square mile in 1840, to 26.3 in 1860.

Few people realize how this abundance of land has simplified all social problems for us in this country. We have laughed at the fear of over-population,—that nightmare of the countries of Europe. There has always been room for the restless and energetic.

When a man failed in the East he could go to the West. When trade became unprofitable, a man could take to agriculture. Our public land has been our great safety-valve, relieving the pressure of economic distress and failure. This enormous expansion has been due very largely to it.

The process of settling this immense territory would, however, have been extremely slow if it had not been for the invention of railroads by which the land was brought within reach of the population of the East and at the same time an outlet provided for the products of the West. Railroads began in 1830. Since that time there have been built over 150,000 miles. They have hastened the material development of the country by many decades. Political unity, also, could scarcely be possible over our immense territory if it were not for these means of communication which have made the Pacific coast as near to Washington as New York was in the old days; or if political unity were possible it would be only by the exercise of despotic power such as the Czar's in Russia.

The third factor in this development has been immigration. Thereby the growth of population has been reinforced by an enormous influx of people from Europe, in the most productive ages of manhood and womanhood, who have not only directly added to the number of inhabitants but have contributed to the power of natural increase. It is an interesting question to determine the amount of this influence and its effect on the race composition of the population of the United States.

If we start with the distinction expressed in the preceding chapter between colonists and immigrants, and draw the line between the two at 1790 or, what would amount to very much the same thing, at 1820, the question would naturally arise: How many of the present inhabitants of the United States are the descendants of the original colonists and how many of the immigrants? It is impossible to answer this question accurately, because we have no statistics of births and deaths for the whole of the United States, and we do not attempt to follow the nationality of the people in our decennial censuses further than the birthplace of the parent. There are, however, one or two ways by which we can estimate the number due to immigration. One is on the basis of the fifteen million people who, according to the census of 1880, were either themselves of foreign birth or the children of parents born abroad. That number represents those immigrants who survived down to 1880 and their children born on this soil. But many of the immigrants who came in the earlier years, say before 1850, are now represented by the third and even by the fourth generation. These should be added to the others. The number of immigrants who arrived before 1850 was nearly 2,500,000. Granting that they are now represented by grandchildren and in some cases by great-grandchildren, and that by the natural increase of each succeeding generation the number would by 1880 have doubled, we have an additional five millions, making about twenty millions in all.

A second method of estimating the number of our population who are of foreign descent has been pointed out by Dr. Edward Jarvis.[1] The basis of his estimate is the two figures of the number of immigrants landing here during each decade and the total population of the United States at each census. For instance take the decade 1870–1880. During that period the white population increased by 9,815,981. There arrived during the decade 2,944,695 immigrants. In 1880 these immigrants had lived here an average of 3.7 years. Allowing them an increase during that period of two per cent per annum, the total number of immigrants and their descendants in 1880 would have been 3,162,502. This would leave 6,653,479 as the natural increase of the white population exclusive of the immigrants, or 19.48 per cent in ten years. This rate of increase applies equally to those of the white population in 1870 who were descendants of colonists and those who were descendants of immigrants. This is, of course, an arbitrary

---

[1] Atlantic Monthly, vol. 29, p. 468 (April, 1872).

assumption, but there appears to be no good reason to suppose that the natural increase of the descendants of the immigrants is any less than that of the descendants of the colonists. In fact when we remember that the majority of these immigrants are in the productive ages of manhood and womanhood, and that they belong to the lower classes, in which the tendency to marry and have large families is greater than among the upper classes, the probability is that they contribute their full share to the growth of the community.

By this same method the natural rate of increase is worked out for each decade back to 1820. Then we can begin at 1790 and taking the immigration and the rate of increase from decade to decade estimate the present number of immigrants and their descendants. Dr. Jarvis, by this method of computation, calculated that in 1870 the number of whites of foreign descent was 11,607,394 and the number of native descent was 21,479,595. Carrying on the same calculation to 1880 it appears that the number of whites of foreign descent was about eighteen millions, and of native descent about twenty-five and one-half millions. Using the rate of increase of the decade 1870–1880 to carry the calculation still further it would appear that by the middle of the year 1888 the whites of foreign descent numbered over twenty-five millions, and of American descent twenty-nine millions. Less than one-half of the total population of the United States are descendants of the original white colonists.

The enormous influence of immigration on the population of the United States is at once seen by these figures. The native white population has increased with wonderful rapidity, for, as we have said, most of the natural restraints on population have not been operative in our past history. But besides this enormous natural increase we have constantly received additional people from the countries of Europe. A writer in the Journal of the London Statistical Society for 1884 has expressed this graphically as follows: Assume the average age of the immigrants on arrival to be twenty years. Suppose that one hundred persons of that age represent the survivors of one hundred and fifty births. These one hundred and fifty births represent the natural increase of a population of six thousand souls. Such an immigration as that of 1882 represents the natural increase of a population of nearly fifty million people. In other words we have a foreign population equal to our own contributing to our growth by its natural increase.

It is not necessary to point out the immense influence which the rapid growth of population due to immigration has had on the material development of this country. It has supplied that labor force which was necessary to bring the soil under cultivation. It has enabled us to take up great stretches of territory. It has built railroads, dug canals, made highways, cut down forests, in short turned the wilderness into cultivated land. It is safe to say that without this immigration the growth of the country would have been very much slower, and that we should only now be where we were twenty years ago. It has quickened the pace of our development and made us do things rapidly and on a large scale. We are apt to attribute our prosperity too much to our own genius and talent. We forget the factors that have worked with us and in our favor. Unlimited land and an army of intelligent workers furnished with the best implements of labor have made great material progress almost necessary.

A much more important subject of study, however, is the effect of this immigration on the ethnical or race composition of our population. If it at present consisted merely of the descendants of the people who were here in 1790, with slight additions from year to year of immigrants from Europe, we should be, with the exception of the blacks, a remarkably homogeneous people. Notwithstanding the fact that among the original colonists were to be found Dutch, Germans, Swedes and French, yet the dominating element was the English. This is seen in the fact that the language has remained English, and that the institutions are English. The long connection of all the colonies with England, whatever the original home of the colonists, accounts for this in large measure. The revolutionary struggle united the people and gave them the feeling of one nationality. Free institutions have worked in the same way, until we find the native born Americans, however widely separated by distance, exhibiting very much the same traits. In later years the means of communication, the common interest in the common government, and still more the commercial intercourse unhindered by tax-barriers and facilitated by the same language, the same money and similar commercial law have unified the whole. There is less difference in language, customs and feeling between the inhabitants of distant portions of the United States than there is often between counties or provinces of European States, which have had different historical development. This influence has been so strong that it has enabled us to assimilate many elements of different quality, and has leavened, at least to a certain extent, the whole lump.

But during the last forty years the immigration has been so large that the process of assimilation has become more difficult, and the addition of foreign elements has been so rapid that it has made the race composition of our population essentially different from what it would have been if we had been left to our own natural growth. These foreign elements are now so prominent that it is worth our while to consider the actual composition of our population as it presents itself to-day. The method of analysis and the results have already been indicated. Our population falls into three groups : — the descendants of the original colonists (whites); the immigrants since 1790 and their descendants; and the negroes. The proportion of the descendants of the immigrants tends to become greater, for they are reinforced not only by the natural increase of those already here but by fresh immigrants and their natural increase. The fact therefore that the proportion of the foreign to the native born was slightly less in 1880 than it was in 1870 shows nothing in regard to the real strength of the foreign born and their descendants in this country. The proportion is vitiated by the fact that the children of immigrants who are born in this country are classed as native born.

It would appear from the figures that alien elements are very strongly represented in our population. The negroes are by birth and race and previous condition of servitude incapable of representing the full American capacity for political and social life. They have neither the traditions of political life nor practical experience in self-government. The presence of this numerous body of people, who will never fully amalgamate with the white population, will always be a problem for us. The tendency will be for them to remain in a position of inferiority, unable fully to meet the demands on their intelligence and virtue which our system of political liberty and equality makes. They are a legacy of the slave period and the nemesis which long years of evasion of our national problem has left with us. We cannot escape the difficulty, and it is only fair to say that they have displayed a docility and good nature since their emancipation which have made them a comparatively harmless, if not progressive and desirable, element in our national life.

We turn now to the consideration of the ethnic influence of the elements added to our population by immigration. This is a much more difficult problem than that of the black race. In the first place, because there is no distinguishing mark, such as color, to separate the foreigners and their descendants from the descendants of the colonists. Even if there is no amalgamation, the very fact that they are all white makes them indistinguishable either by the census or by common observation. We have already seen how difficult it is to determine even the total number of the descendants of immigrants now living in this country. But in the second place there is a real amalgamation going on which renders the descendant of the immigrant in many cases practically identical with the native American in capacity, feeling and national characteristics. It would be absurd to treat the whole twenty or twenty-five millions whom we have reckoned to be of foreign descent as alien elements in our civilization. Many of these persons have been born on our soil and know no other country and no other language or institutions than ours. They are as truly American in thought and feeling as any descendant of the Puritan fathers. Even where they have come to this country poor, ignorant and perhaps vicious, they have seized upon the chance to begin a new life and have elevated themselves and their children to a higher plane of civilization. Economic well-being and the practice of free institutions are the most powerful agents of civilization.

There are, now, three figures which will give us some notion of the strength and character of this foreign influence. One is the statistics of immigration according to nationality; a second is the number of persons of foreign parentage,—that is, who were either born abroad or whose parents were born abroad; the third is the number of persons now living in this country who were actually born abroad. Each one of these figures is incomplete in itself as an index of the influence of immigration, but each supplements the others; and by a skilful interweaving of the facts indicated by the three we can arrive at some appreciation of this great movement.

The foreign element in the United States is composed of many different nationalities, and the first step is to determine the relative proportions of these. Since the year 1820 more than fifteen million immigrants have landed on our shores. Of these 3,387,279 came from Ireland; 1,529,792, from England and Wales; 312,924, from Scotland; 4,359,121, from Germany; 857,083, from Norway and Sweden; 127,642, from Denmark; 357,333, from France; 160,201, from Switzerland; 320,796, from Italy. The principal elements added to our population are German and Irish, with a strong mixture also of Scotch, Scandinavian and, in recent years, a considerable number of Italians.

Statistics for successive years show that the character of the movement is undergoing considerable change. The relative number of the Irish is decreasing and that of the Germans is increasing. During the decade 1841–1850 the Irish formed 45.57 per cent of the whole number of immigrants; from 1871 to 1880 they were only 15.10 per cent. On the other hand the Germans, who formed in 1841–1850, 25.37 per cent of the whole number, in 1851–60 were 36.63 per cent, in 1861–1870 were 33.32 per cent, and in 1871–1880 still 25.74 per cent. The relative number from the smaller nationalities such as Norway and Sweden, Italy and Austria-Hungary tends constantly to increase.

About the same distribution of ethnic elements is seen in the statistics of foreign parentage at the tenth census. Taking the birthplace of the father as a test, it appeared that there were in the United States:

4,883,842 persons having German fathers.
4,529,523 persons having Irish fathers.
2,039,808 persons having British fathers.
  635,405 persons having Scandinavian fathers.
  939,247 persons having British American fathers.
1,321,485 persons having fathers born in other foreign countries.
  573,434 persons having native fathers and foreign mothers.

It appears from this that the ethnic element most powerfully influencing the population of the United States at the present time is the German, and that next to it comes the Irish. When we consider, however, that there are over two million persons having British fathers and mothers, most of them English; that there are over six hundred thousand Scandinavians who are of pure Germanic blood; and that a part of the British Americans would also be English (although a part of them would doubtless be French and Irish), it will appear that the Germanic influence is still dominant in the formation of the population of the United States.

The statistics of the foreign born in the tenth census present very much the same picture. Of the 6,679,943 persons of foreign birth, 1,966,742 were born in Germany; 1,854,571 in Ireland; 662,676 in England; 170,136 in Scotland; 717,157 in British America; 194,337 in Sweden; 181,729 in Norway; 106,971 in France, etc. The importance of the Germanic element is seen in these figures.

If we follow out these foreign elements we shall find that they are very differently distributed throughout the United States. They are much stronger in the North than in the South; different nationalities tend to concentrate themselves in particular states; and the foreigners are as a rule more numerous in the cities than in the country. All of these things are clearly disclosed by the statistics of the tenth census.

The record of the avowed destination of immigrants landing at the port of New York presents a very curious picture of the influences already felt by the immigrants almost before they have landed. For instance, of the 371,619 immigrants who arrived in the year 1887, New England was the avowed destination of 24,510; the Middle States of 219,836; the Western States of 100,347; the Pacific States and the Territories of 16,371; and the Southern States of 4,651. No very great stress can be laid on these figures, because in many cases the immigrants have no definite intention as to where they will settle. Thus not less than 151,023 avowed their intention of settling in New York. Of course many of these afterwards moved on to other states.[1]

The tenth census showed similar results in the distribution of the foreign born. In 1880 the New England States contained 793,612 persons of foreign birth; the Middle States, 2,130,304; the Western States, 2,916,829; the Pacific States and the Territories, 614,678; and the Southern States, 224,520. The reasons for this distribution are sufficiently obvious. For many years slavery kept free labor out of the Southern States, and so they received but a small part of the immigration. The factory towns, the large cities and the mines attracted the unskilled labor to the New England and Middle States; while the unlimited land attracted the greatest number to the West.

The nationalities show their aptitudes in the choice of localities in which to settle. The Irish stay largely in the great cities or in factory towns, and so we find them represented heavily in Massachusetts (226,700), in New York (499,445), Pennsylvania (236,505), Illinois (117,343), New Jersey, Connecticut and Rhode Island. The Germans stay to a certain extent in large cities, and we find them, too, in New York (355,913), Pennsylvania (168,426), Illinois and Missouri. The Germans are also farmers and we find them in Ohio, Wisconsin, Michigan and Iowa. The

---

[1] New York Commissioners of Emigration, Report for 1887.

English are found in the mines of Pennsylvania as well as in the city of New York. The British Americans are in the factories of Massachusetts and in the lumber forests of Michigan — and in fact all along the frontier. The Scandinavians have founded their own colonies in Minnesota and Wisconsin.

The strength of this foreign element is disclosed if we take a typical state and study the make-up of its population more closely. Massachusetts is commonly thought of as peculiarly an American community, where the population is largely composed of descendants of the Puritans. It was found in 1885 that over twenty-seven per cent of the inhabitants of that commonwealth were of foreign birth, and that over one-half of all the inhabitants were of foreign parentage. Nearly thirty per cent were of Irish parentage alone.

The persons of foreign birth in the United States seem to seek the large cities. In 1880 more than thirty-four per cent were found therein. Of the Irish, forty-five per cent settle in the large cities; of the Germans, thirty-eight per cent; of the English and Scotch, thirty per cent; of the Italians, sixty per cent. In the city of Boston in 1885 only thirty-one per cent of the inhabitants were of native (*i.e.* born in the United States) parentage; the rest were of foreign parentage. In the city of Lowell only thirty per cent were of native parentage; in Lawrence, twenty-two per cent; in Fall River, seventeen per cent; and in the city of Holyoke, only sixteen per cent. Many of our factory towns and cities are really foreign so far as the nationality of their inhabitants goes.

These statistics show that in certain parts of the country the foreign element in our population has become very powerful and is in fact overshadowing the native. Especially in the cities it shows its strength. But it always tends to concentrate. This is due to several causes. One is that the immigrants naturally seek that portion of the country where they can find employment in their particular trades. The miners from Wales and England naturally go to the mines of Pennsylvania. The lumbermen from Canada seek the forests of the Northern States. The unskilled labor remains in the large city where it is employed in the rougher parts of building trades, or seeks the factory town where it can soon learn to manage the simple operations of industrial machinery. Another great influence is the presence of friends or countrymen upon whom the newly arrived immigrants can depend for help and counsel. Many come at the solicitation of friends or relatives, or with the aid of money sent by them, and naturally go to them on their arrival.

There are, fortunately, certain forces which tend to counteract this exclusiveness on the part of the immigrants and gradually to fuse the different elements into one American nationality. Two of these we have already mentioned, viz., economic prosperity and the practice of free political institutions. The former widens the circle of wants of the new citizen and leads him to imitate the higher style of living which he sees about him. This separates him from the habits and traditions of his native country and he adopts new standards which are associated in his mind with the new domicile, and which produce a feeling of superiority when he revisits the old home or comes into contact with later arrivals. It differentiates him, so to speak, from the immigrant, and gives him a feeling of attachment to the country where he has prospered. This feeling increases with his children and grandchildren until they become fully identified with our customs, manner of living and habits of thought, and are thoroughly Americanized.

The exercise of political rights, to which many of the immigrants are strange, tends to differentiate them in much the same way. It makes them of importance to the political leaders. It gives them a higher position than they were accustomed to at home, and this naturally attaches them to the new country. However much our politics may suffer from the addition of this vote, much of it ignorant and some of it depraved, there is no doubt as to the educational and nationalizing effect of the suffrage on the immigrants themselves. However attached the Irishman may be to the cause of home rule for Ireland, or however proud the German may be of the military glory of the empire, his feelings must gradually and unconsciously gravitate to the country where he has found economic prosperity and political recognition. He may still observe the national feast days and wave the old flag, but if it ever came to a contest, he would probably find that he was more of an American than an Irishman or a German.

Another great fusing force has been the dominance of one language,—the English. In the great mass of cases the immigrant has found it necessary or desirable to adopt that language. Where he has not done it himself, his children have; and in many cases it has become the mother tongue if not the only tongue of the descendants. As soon as that happens, the man of foreign descent is irreparably separated from his former home. In some cases thickly settled communities have managed to maintain the foreign speech and the old religion for several generations. But the disintegrating forces are at work all about them. The moment the young man ventures out into the world he is obliged to learn English. The moment he aspires to the higher education or to political or commercial position he must recognize the prevailing tongue. The children learn it in the school. The parents recognize that it is desirable for the children if not for themselves. It is impossible to isolate the little community completely and it is gradually undermined.

It is eminently desirable that it should be so. We must have one speech in this country. We must insist that English shall be taught in the schools and that it shall be the fundamental language of future generations. It must be everywhere the official language of the courts and the laws. German clergymen and educated men sometimes regret that the immigrants and their descendants should lose this connection with the old country and access to the great literature of the German tongue. But it is better that a man should have one country and not divide his allegiance. If we are to build up in this country one nationality we must insist upon one speech.

There is one other way in which the foreign elements might amalgamate with each other and with the native, so as in the course of time to form one homogeneous people,—that is by intermarriage. In the case of the blacks there is the insuperable color obstacle in the way of their fusion with the whites. But in the case of the immigrants this does not exist, and the impediments of difference in language, customs, and even religion may gradually be removed. It is a question of great interest how far such a fusion of blood is actually occurring in the United States.

The statistics on this point are not very encouraging to those persons who believe that mixture of blood in the United States will finally produce a race different from and superior to any of the older nationalities. It appears that where a particular nationality is concentrated in any one locality, the men choose wives of their own race. For instance, out of 10,000 Irishmen living in the city of New York 9,441 had wives who were born in Ireland, 393 had native born wives, 119 had wives born in Great Britain, 13 had German wives, etc. The same fact is true of the Germans in New York or wherever they are heavily represented, of the Scandinavians in Minnesota and Wisconsin, etc. On the other hand where the nationality is poorly represented the men often take wives from other nationalities. For instance, of 10,000 Irishmen in Maryland not less than 1,247 had wives of native birth.[1] It is to be observed that these statistics are not very conclusive because they include marriages that were contracted on the other side, when of course there was no choice open.

---

[1] The immigrants of British birth or descent show the greatest inclination to marry native women, — obviously because there is no obstacle of language. The same thing is true of the British-American except in the New England States where the French-Canadians are included under this designation. The very interesting and curious tables relating to this subject may be found in the Tenth Census of the United States, vol. 1, p. 677. See also Massachusetts Census of 1885, vol. 1, part 1, p. 673.

They are principally the marriages of the first generation where it would be natural to marry in the same nationality. It is possible that the future generations of different blood may intermarry more freely. But even here it is seen how desirable it is to break up the concentration of immigrants of the same nationality in one place, so that by intermarriage with the natives and with people of other nationality this process of fusion and amalgamation may be hastened.

It is one of the favorite theories of social philosophers that mixed races are the strongest. And it is true as a matter of history that the most progressive peoples of Europe are mixed in blood. The American people of the future will be a race composed of many different elements, and it is possible that this mixture will have produced a people possessing the best characteristics displayed by these various elements. It seems, however, that there are two things that ought to be carefully considered. One is that the constituent elements of this amalgamation should themselves be of desirable quality. It is scarcely probable that by taking the dregs of Europe we shall produce a people of high social intelligence and morality. The second is that we must see to it that the opportunity for amalgamation is really given. Simply placing these discordant elements in juxtaposition will not make a compact and solid whole. On the contrary it will give rise to an atomistic weakness which will make any homogeneous and harmonious development impossible. A nation is great, not on account of the number of individuals contained within its boundaries, but through the strength begotten of common national ideals and aspirations. No nation can exist and be powerful that is not homogeneous in this sense. And the great ethnic problem we have before us is to fuse these diverse elements into one common nationality, having one language, one political practice, one patriotism and one ideal of social development.

CHAPTER V.

THE POLITICAL EFFECTS OF IMMIGRATION.

It is obvious that the enormous influx of immigrants during the last thirty or forty years must have had a great effect on political life in this country. Whatever the character of the immigrants, it is not probable that they have had the same political traditions and training as the descendants of the original settlers. Through the institution of universal suffrage and the short naturalization period, this influence is very soon measured by their numerical strength, without regard to their education, character or ability. In no state or territory does the number of foreign born equal the native born, but in many cases it bears a large proportion to the latter. And if we take into account the foreign parentage, the proportion is still greater. Indeed, in some localities, especially in large cities, the persons of foreign parentage fairly overwhelm those of native descent.

Again, the proportion of native to foreign born does not fully represent the political strength of the latter. Among the foreign born there is always an abnormal proportion of males and of adults. This is already disclosed in the bare figures of immigration, where sixty per cent are males and seventy-five per cent are above the age of fifteen. So in Massachusetts, while of the native born only 54.5 per cent are twenty years of age and over, of the foreign born 84.5 per cent are of that age. The same thing is shown by the census of 1880. At that time the males of twenty-one years and over (voting population) constituted 25.5 per cent of the total population of the United States; the native born white males of that age constituted 22.4 per cent of the native white population; while the foreign born white males of twenty-one years and over constituted 46 per cent of the foreign born white population.

It is true that all these persons do not vote. Some of them have not been here long enough to be naturalized, some neglect the opportunity, and others are incapacitated for various reasons. The census of Massachusetts (1885) gave a very curious table showing for each nationality the proportion of males above the age of twenty who were still aliens, — that is, who had not become naturalized. The Irish are most eager to become naturalized, the English and Scotch much less so, and the French Canadians, Italians and Portuguese least so. In these latter cases it is evidently because they have been here an insufficient length of time, or because the difficulties of the language and the general indifference to the exercise of political power make it less desired by them. As soon, however, as this vote becomes numerous enough to be worth controlling, it will doubtless be naturalized and utilized by unscrupulous politicians and party managers.

It is a curious fact that only in recent years has the increase of this foreign vote excited any apprehension or even jealousy on the part of the native born voters. We have quietly received and absorbed this addition to our electorate without making any effort to prepare it for its new duties. There has never been any decided movement against it. On the contrary, the tendency has been to make the conditions of suffrage more and more easy and to admit foreigners to it on the same footing as the natives. It is true that we had alien and sedition laws as early as 1798–99, but they were purely political moves and had no reference to immigration which was then in its infancy. So also there was an American or Know-Nothing party in 1854, but that was really a No-Popery excitement and quickly died out.[1] We have followed the principle of incorporating the new comers with the body politic as soon as possible and then treating them exactly like native citizens. They are admitted to all public offices with

---

[1] As late as 1866 a Congressional committee on immigration reported that the immigrants were a most valuable acquisition to this country.

the exception of the presidency and vice-presidency of the United States.

From the broadest point of view this has been wise policy. It has prevented the formation of a servile class in this country or of any well-defined system of classes. It has offered every inducement to the immigrant to make the most of himself. It has carried out logically our ideas of political liberty and equality, and we have secured all the advantages that pure democracy can offer. Until very recent years the power of assimilation has apparently been sufficient to carry on this process without any serious break-down of the political machinery. Of late, however, there are signs that the task is becoming more difficult and that we are suffering under serious evils due to this constant addition to our voting population of persons not altogether fitted to exercise the right of suffrage. Some of these indications are as follows:

Our liberality in conferring political privileges on aliens has resulted in destroying every test of the qualification of immigrants for the exercise of political rights. The naturalization act now in force is practically that passed in 1802. The requirements of this act are:— 1. Preliminary declaration three years before admission (modified in some cases); 2. Proof of five years' residence in the United States and one year's residence in the state; 3. Proof of good conduct, attachment to the principles of the constitution, etc.; 4. Renunciation of any title of nobility; 5. Declaration, on oath or affirmation, that he (the person desiring admission) will support the constitution of the United States, and that he abjures his former allegiance. The evident intention of this act was to admit all persons of good character, who came to this country with the intention of staying here, to all the rights and privileges of American citizens. We have in fact gone so far as to advocate expatriation as a natural right against the law of all European states, including the common law of England, and we have effectually protected the rights of naturalized citizens of the United States by the expatriation treaties of 1868 and the following years.

But the curious thing is that in practice the test provided and the proof required in regard to good conduct and attachment to the principles of the constitution have become a dead letter. The courts have made them a merely formal matter, and any alien who has been here the required length of time and complied with the requirement as to previous declaration of intention, and who can bring one or two persons who will say that he is of good character, is at once admitted to citizenship. In the enormous number of applicants every year, it would be impossible for the court to test the character of each very thoroughly; but it seems to have become the custom not to attempt any such examination, the court contenting itself with the formal procedure noted above. In some cases the clerk conducts the examination, while the court is busy with other matters. Any court, either state or federal, can naturalize aliens, so that the states have authority over this matter which is of national importance. So also the right to exercise the suffrage does not depend upon naturalization, although it generally accompanies it, but is determined by state legislation. In fourteen states the foreigner is allowed to vote for members of the state legislature, and consequently for members of Congress, after he has declared his intention of becoming naturalized, although he has never applied for naturalization and never may. In some states only one year's residence is required and that need not be the year previous to naturalization. Often the applicant can neither read nor write. What can he know about the Constitution of the United States?[1]

We are thus conferring the privilege of citizenship, including the right to vote, without any test of the man's fitness for it. There seems to be no reason why we should not make the test a real one, and unhesitatingly reject those who through ignorance

[1] Justice William Strong in the North American Review, vol. 138, p. 418 (1884).

or depravity are unfit for the exercise of political rights. One or two recent court decisions show a tendency on the part of the judges to carry out the spirit of the statute instead of complying simply with the letter.[1]

[1] One of these decisions was rendered by Judge Daniels of the New York Supreme Court. Upon a close examination of an applicant for naturalization before him and the usual witnesses, the fact was brought out that the applicant was in the habit of becoming intoxicated at no great recurring intervals of time, and while in that condition of abusing his wife and family, and that he had on several occasions been arrested and punished therefor. Judge Daniels refused the application for naturalization on the ground that the applicant was not proved to have behaved as a man of good moral character, well disposed to the good order and happiness of the United States as required by the United States Revised Statutes. He said: "This privilege of citizenship has been provided as a reward for good behavior and demonstrated attachment to the principles of free government. The design of the law is, in great part, certainly to induce and secure the co-operation of all the persons residing in the United States in supporting the laws and Constitution of the country. But this fidelity to its interests and progress is not to be expected from and will not be supplied by disorderly and dissipated persons. Reliance cannot be placed upon them for the support of the principles of free government or the enforcement of good order or the laws enacted to secure and promote it. They cannot therefore be held to be persons who have behaved themselves as persons of good moral character, and without that they are not permitted by the statutes to become citizens of the United States." In another case which came up in the Philadelphia Court of Common Pleas the applicant, a Hungarian, when asked to take the oath of allegiance declared that he did not believe in a deity of any kind and that he neither swore nor affirmed. His application was refused. Both these decisions seem to manifest a tendency on the part of the courts to scrutinize more closely the qualifications of foreigners for naturalization. Bradstreet's, September 29, 1888.

One consequence of the admission of this mass of foreigners to political power before they have become thoroughly assimilated with our body politic is seen in the attempt to win the foreign (particularly the Irish and German) vote. These naturalized citizens retain certain prejudices in respect to their old home, or have ideas not in unison with those of the mass of American citizens about them. The Irish demand that we shall conduct our foreign policy according to the relations of England to Ireland, and that we shall protect naturalized citizens in acts hostile to a power with which we are on terms of friendship. Politicians yield to these prejudices, and our politics are debauched by the attempt to win these votes. The German vote in many localities controls the action of political leaders on the liquor question, oftentimes being in opposition to the sentiment of the native community. It is a bad thing that our political life should be controlled by the prejudices of a single nationality of newly arrived immigrants. It prevents questions being decided on their merits. It introduces motives which have nothing to do with the question of the prosperity and the advantage of the country at large. It is possible that one might include here the power exercised in our politics by the Roman Catholic church, based on this power of suffrage vested in persons who vote according to the commands of the priests. It is not easy to trace this out closely, but there is no doubt that such power has been exercised in times past in the state of New York for the purpose of getting public money and lands for church purposes. Residence in this country seems to weaken the hold of the church on its male members. But the mischief is done by admitting these men to vote before the solvent power of American life has had time to loosen the bonds of priestly authority, and before they have absorbed our notions of freedom of conscience and absolute separation of church and state. There would have been no trouble as it is, if it had not been for the increasing number of immigrants, which makes this uneducated and un-American vote so powerful. The combination of the number and the docility of this vote makes it dangerous to our institutions.

The bad influence of a purely ignorant vote is seen in the degradation of our municipal administrations in America. The foreign born congregate in the large cities, especially the mass of unskilled laborers. There they easily come under the control of leaders of their own nation who use their voting power for the purpose of getting possession of the city government and administering it for the sake of the money to be made out of it. Places in the municipal service are filled with political workers, and city contracts are jobbed out to political supporters. This indirect bribery rapidly develops into direct buying of votes at the polls. The evil does not stop with a bad and extravagant administration of city affairs. State elections and even national issues become entangled in the same vicious connection, until the highest officers of the national government may owe their election to some corrupt municipal leader and be obliged to acknowledge the obligation and cancel it by appointments to office after election.

Another indication of the unfortunate effect of introducing so many men of foreign birth and belief into our social body is seen in the recent outbreaks of anarchism and socialism. These movements are always led and for the most part carried on by persons of foreign birth. Socialism and anarchism are not plants of American growth nor of Anglo-Saxon origin. They are not natural to the American mind; neither are they due to any deterioration in the condition of the laboring class in this country, and thus the fruit of despair and hopelessness in regard to the future. They are the importations of foreign agitators who come here for the purpose of making converts to their doctrines. These men are under false impressions as to the rights of liberty which they shall enjoy here, and they interpret the freedom of agitation and of speech which we allow them as evidences of the weakness of our government. And in fact we have so long been accustomed to permit the individual to air his grievances, depending upon the common-sense of the mass of the people to distinguish the true from the false, that we are ill prepared to cope with men who do not hesitate to resort to conspiracy and revolutionary violence. We have been accustomed to rely upon the general respect for law which prevails in a democracy where the law is the rule of the majority. In these agitators we have characters of a different stamp, men who use freedom for the purpose of conspiring social revolution by violence.

These outbreaks have a grave significance in another respect. They indicate a change of sentiment towards the institutions of this country. In former times, — thirty or forty years ago, — the immigrants regarded our republic as the model of a free government. They rejoiced in their escape from the monarchies of Europe, and came here enthusiastic for democratic institutions. To-day the socialist and the anarchist look upon the republic as entirely inadequate to fulfil their ideal of what a state ought to be. They are as far in advance of us as we have supposed ourselves to be in advance of the absolute monarchy. They desire the overthrow of all social institutions, of state, of property, of inheritance, of marriage and of religion. Their views are incompatible with social and political institutions as we regard them. There is and must be an irreconcilable conflict between their success and the maintenance of existing civilization. The two cannot live together.

But however willing we may be to acquiesce in reform and modification of institutions in order to meet the changing conditions of the age, yet there are certain "fundamentals" in every social system, to destroy which destroys the system itself. Our institutions have grown up with us and are adapted to our national character and needs. To change them in accordance with the demands of agitators who have no knowledge of that character and those needs would be absurd and destructive. It is putting politics on the worst of all "a priori" bases. It is neglecting all the teachings of experience and adopting the theoretical views of men of another civilization, brought up under the influence of other ideas. Most of these men have been trained under the paternal system of governmental restraint and supervision of the actions of the individual. They have no idea of the independence and self-reliance of the American character, the result of many years of self-government and taking care of one's self. The economic and political philosophy adapted to them is entirely different from that adapted to an English-speaking race.

But these men, ignorant of our institutions, hostile

to them and plotting their overthrow, we not only admit freely to the country but grant to them freedom of speech and of meeting, and in a few years invite them to share in political power. It cannot be but that we should feel the effect on the smooth working of democratic institutions which have for their pre-condition the understanding that the mass of the community are in favor of them and are satisfied with them. Even if we admit these men to the country they should be held responsible before the criminal law; and there is absolutely no need that they should be given a share in that government which they do not understand, and which not understanding they pretend to despise and condemn.[1]

[1] Prof. James Bryce in his American Commonwealth thinks that immigration "is not so largely answerable for the faults of American politics as the stranger might be led by the language of many Americans to believe. . . . The cities have no doubt suffered from the immigrant vote. But New York was not an Eden before the Irish came; and would not become an Eden were they all to move on to San Francisco." Vol. 2, p. 261. Yet Mr. Bryce speaks in many places of the strain put on political institutions by this constant immigration; for instance: "The immigrants vote, . . . but they are not fit for the suffrage. They know nothing of the institutions of the country, of its statesmen, of its political issues. Neither from Germany nor from Ireland do they bring much knowledge of the methods of free government. . . . Such a sacrifice of common sense to abstract principles has seldom been made by any country. . . . A stranger must not presume to say that the Americans have been imprudent, but he may doubt whether the possible ultimate gain compensates the direct and certain danger." Vol. 2, p. 67. See also pp. 260, 261, 267, 270, 328, and 710.

It is in these respects that unrestricted immigration is affecting our political life. Years ago when the annual arrivals were small and the total number of foreigners insignificant compared with the native population, the strain was not felt. But as the number has increased and the character of the additions to the electorate has not improved but deteriorated, and as this hostility to our social institutions has displayed itself, the strain has become increasingly difficult to bear. It is a serious question how long democratic institutions can stand such a test. The demand of the individual for privileges and enjoyments is becoming more and more vociferous. The duty of the individual to the social organization and his obligation to the social order become less and less emphasized, until it appears as if all political life were about to resolve itself into a selfish struggle for personal advantage. We have not simplified but enormously complicated the evolution of our social life by the addition of so many heterogeneous and discordant elements.

CHAPTER VI.

THE ECONOMIC GAIN BY IMMIGRATION.[1]

UNRESTRICTED immigration has been defended on two grounds — the one ideal, the other practical. Freedom of migration is sometimes asserted to be a natural right of man, or at least one of the products of political liberty with which we have no business to interfere. Coupled with this argument the notion frequently appears that this country was destined to be an asylum for the oppressed of all nations, and that to restrict their coming would be to prove faithless to our duty. On the other hand, perfect freedom of immigration has been defended and encouraged on the ground of the immense economic advantage of this constant addition to the labor force of the community. It is proposed to deal in this chapter with the second of these considerations.

It has already been pointed out that the wonderful growth of this country is due in large measure to the constant additions to our productive laboring population by immigration. Thereby we have been en-

[1] A portion of this chapter has already been printed in the Political Science Quarterly for June, 1888.

abled to occupy and settle the lands of the West. It is true that the immigrants do not take to agriculture as readily as they do to mining and mechanical industries, possibly on account of the capital required to purchase and stock a farm, but they are found in large numbers engaged as agricultural laborers and in kindred occupations. The census of 1880 returned nearly 800,000 persons of foreign birth as engaged in agriculture, over ten per cent of the whole number so engaged. In the Western States the proportion is much larger. In Minnesota, for instance, over one-half of those engaged in agriculture were of foreign birth. In the state of Michigan in 1887, according to an investigation by the bureau of labor statistics, of some 90,000 farmers in that state over one-third were of foreign birth. In all the Western States there are communities composed entirely of immigrants and their descendants. The Scandinavians, especially, take to farming; and large numbers of British Americans are engaged in the lumber industry.

The exploitation of our mineral wealth has been due largely to the immigrants, — over one-half of the men employed in mining in 1880 being persons of foreign birth. It is this unskilled but hardy labor that has enabled us to open up our immense country with railroads; and over one-quarter of the employees of these railroads at the present time are of foreign birth. It is scarcely possible to see how we could have accomplished this work without immigration.

So also after the country has been opened up, it is the foreign born who have aided in its development by working in factories and in mechanical industries of all sorts, besides furnishing us with domestic servants. Nearly one-third of all the persons engaged in manufacturing, mechanical and mining industries in 1880 were of foreign birth. In our cotton mills, 45 per cent of the operatives were of foreign birth; in our woollen mills, 39 per cent; in our paper mills, 33 per cent; in our iron and steel works, 36 per cent; among our curriers and leather dressers, 45 per cent; among our engineers and firemen, 27 per cent; and so on through almost the entire list of factory operatives. Even in the small mechanical trades we are dependent on the foreign born. Among our bakers 56 per cent are foreign born; among our blacksmiths, 27 per cent; among our boot and shoemakers, 36 per cent; among our butchers, 38 per cent; among the carpenters and joiners, 23 per cent; among the cigar makers, 44 per cent; among the coopers, 33 per cent; among the masons, 35 per cent; among the plasterers, 27 per cent, etc. Many of these crafts have gone very largely into the hands of foreigners.[1]

In many of the Western States nearly one-half of

[1] Tenth Census of the United States, vol. 2, Manufactures.

all the persons engaged in manufacturing, mechanical and mining industries are of foreign birth; for instance, in Minnesota, 47.5 per cent; in Wisconsin, 48.8 per cent; in Illinois, 43.3 per cent; in Michigan, 43.4 per cent, etc. In the heavily manufacturing states of the East even, the number of employees of foreign birth is extremely large. In Massachusetts it was 35.6 per cent; in Rhode Island, 39.1 per cent; in New York, 38.7 per cent; and in Connecticut, 32.4 per cent.

The census of 1880 showed a great army of workers who were born abroad engaged in adding to the wealth of the United States. There were over a million Germans, nearly a million Irish, four hundred and fifty thousand British, three hundred and fifty thousand British Americans, two hundred thousand Scandinavians, and four hundred and fifty thousand foreigners of other nationalities. We may well ask what we should have done and what we should now do if it were not for these workers. It must also be remembered that there are thousands of laborers who are the children of immigrants, who are not included in these figures.

While admitting that immigration has been one of the most important factors in our past development and that without it our national progress would certainly have been much slower, yet it does not follow that further immigration is necessary or even a distinct economic gain. In former times, with our undeveloped resources and our unoccupied territory, any addition to our labor force of whatever character was a distinct gain. Now, however, we are beyond that first necessity. We have a population of sixty millions, the natural increase of which must be between a million and a million and a half a year; this would seem to be quite sufficient to give us additional labor force as it is needed.

It behooves us, therefore, to consider more carefully the exact economic gain by immigration under our present conditions, when we do not absolutely need the immigrants and can exercise some freedom of choice in admitting them. It is not good statesmanship nor good political science to go on trusting to the generalizations of a quarter or a half a century ago when conditions were entirely different.

The economic gain to us by immigration is of two kinds. First there is the money or capital which the immigrants bring with them; and secondly there is the economic value of the immigrants themselves. Is it possible to calculate what these items amount to?

The immigrants bring with them a considerable amount of money. Each one sells what he has in the old country, and brings the proceeds in the shape of gold or drafts or goods to be invested in the new. In this way there is a constant stream of capital flowing from Europe to the United States which never appears in the statistics of imports, and which has to be offset by no exports. This is a clear economic gain, and when the immigration is heavy this invisible supply of wealth is very considerable and adds to our general prosperity. Various attempts have been made to ascertain how much this sum amounts to. In 1856 the immigrants who landed at the port of New York were asked how much money they had with them, and the average was $68.08 *per capita*. It was said at the time that this amount was probably too small, because many of the immigrants would suspect that the question was asked from some fiscal motive and would put the amount too low. Mr. Friedrich Kapp, one of the commissioners of emigration, estimated that the amount brought by each immigrant was at least $100. This would indicate that there was an annual movement of thirty or forty or fifty millions of gold to this country, which did not appear in the balance of trade — no inconsiderable sum. At the present time Kapp's estimate is probably too large. Our immigrants come more and more from the poorer classes of society, so that the sum *per capita* brought in 1856 is probably no longer brought. We have some German estimates which indicate a smaller sum; and whatever the Germans bring, it is probable that the Irish, the Italians, the Hungarians, etc., bring still less. The latest German authority[1] estimates that the emigrants take with them from 300 to 400 marks each, that is from $75 to $100. An Italian able to raise that sum of money for each member of his family would never think of leaving home.

It must be granted, however, that the immigrants do bring with them a certain amount of wealth, although that amount is probably not very large at the present time. Against this, two things are to be taken into consideration. One is that the inflow of gold into this country is offset by the outflow due to remittances to friends abroad. These remittances are either for the purpose of supporting those who have been left behind, or of paying their passage to this country. Their exact amount has never been ascertained, as they go for the most part through the hands of private bankers or steamship companies. The British Board of Trade printed, for many years, in the "Statistical Tables relating to Emigration and Immigration from and into the United Kingdom," a table of the amount of such remittances, furnished through the courtesy of certain bankers and mercantile houses. The tables are not at all complete, for there is no means of ascertaining the amount transmitted through private parties, and

[1] Becker, Unsere Verluste durch Wanderung, in Schmoller's Jahrbücher, XI, S. 776.

firms unwilling to make a return.[1] Since 1848 no less than £32,294,596 have been thus sent back by settlers in the United States and British North America. In the year 1886 the amount was £1,276,533. The number of emigrants of British and Irish origin going to the United States and British North America during that year was 1,77,455, so that in place of the money each emigrant took out with him we know that a sum equal to $35 was returned. We must also remember that there is a tide of returning immigration. Many of the emigrants, after they have acquired what to them is a competence, return to pass the remainder of their days in the old country. All these returning emigrants carry money with them, and often, doubtless, large sums. Thus in 1886 there were not less than 60,076 persons of British and Irish origin who returned to the United Kingdom from the United States and British North America. This would leave a net emigration of 117,379, and the money taken by each of these emigrants would be offset by a known sum of $52.84. Is it not probable that the balance is against the United States?[2]

There is one other way of looking at this matter,

---

[1] These tables were discontinued in 1888 for that reason.

[2] "Dr. Tuke affirms that the amount sent to Ireland by emigrants every year exceeds the total yearly cost of poor relief in Ireland. And in England too we know that many old people are maintained

when one is inclined to regard every dollar of money that the immigrants bring with them as so much gain to the United States. This has been suggested by the efforts of a German statistician to prove that the loss by emigration is not so great as it seems to be. Dr. Becker[1] remarks that when an emigrant takes 300 or 400 marks out of the country with him, he is not really taking his share of the national fortune. The *per capita* wealth of Germany is at least 3000 or 4000 marks, so that the sum each emigrant takes with him is only one-tenth part of the average national wealth. So long as emigration does not cripple the power of production, it simply leaves a proportionately larger share of the national wealth for every one who remains. If we turn to this country we shall meet the reverse phenomenon. The average wealth in this country must be at least $1000 *per capita*. What does it mean when we add to the number of our citizens thousands who possess only $100 each? Is the country by that fact alone better or worse off? The sum total of wealth has been increased, but the average well-being of the community has been decreased. These men add to the cost

---

out of the savings of their descendants in the colonies." Lord Monkswell in The Fortnightly Review, March, 1888.

The Italian Vice-Consul at New York reported that $4,825,000 had been sent to Italy from the United States alone, in 1883. Rosmini in Il Giornale degli Economisti, July, 1888.

[1] In the article cited above.

of the social organization, while they do not bring the property which is to pay the taxes to defray the expenses of such organization. In a club there is always an initiation fee for new members; and as the club increases in prosperity and wealth this initiation fee is often raised with the perfectly just feeling that it is worth more to belong to the club now than when it was started. It will be said that the immigrant gives himself to the new country and thus pays his initiation fee. In that case the amount of money he brings with him is utterly insignificant. If he is worth having, it makes but little difference whether he brings money with him or not. If he is not worth having, the paltry sum he brings does not begin to pay for the risk of receiving him.

The real economic gain to the United States by immigration consists in the value of the full-grown labor supplied to it by the countries of Europe. Every person passes through two periods of life,— that of unproductive childhood when he is only a burden to the community, and that of productive manhood when he not only supports himself but reimburses the community for the cost of bringing him up. The longer this second period compared with the first, the better for the community; for the total cost of the unproductive period is spread over a greater number of years. The larger the number of persons in this second period compared with the first, the lighter the burden upon the community; for it is shared by a larger number of persons. Of the immigrants into the United States, about 20 per cent are below the age of fifteen, about 70 per cent are between the ages of fifteen and forty, and the remaining 10 per cent are above the age of forty. In other words, four-fifths of the immigrants are in the second period, that of productive manhood, and the great mass of them in the most productive part of that period, that of early manhood. These full-grown laborers have been brought up by the countries of Europe and then presented to us able to support themselves and others. When one considers that the main effort of the world, after all, is to keep itself alive and to provide a future generation to take the place of the present, the economic value of such a gift is enormous. It is like a workman having the latest and best tools provided for him without expense while he is paid for the increased product on the same basis as if he had made the improvements.

It would be absurd to contend that such a movement as we have depicted — the bodily transference of such a labor force from one country to another — has no economic significance. We study with care the statistics of imports and exports; we watch with interest the movements of the precious metals; we encourage industry by artificial tariff regulations; and we are quite sure that all these things have an important influence on the prosperity of the community. Is it not probable that this shifting of labor is as important in its influence on the happiness of the community as the balance of trade or the fluctuations in the rate of discount? No one can deny that; but it is necessary that we take care to judge this influence rightly and measure its force correctly.

Various attempts have been made to express in figures the economic value of the immigrant. The most common estimate of this sort and the one most widely known is due to Mr. Friedrich Kapp.[1] He values the immigrant simply at the cost of bringing him up. Kapp found an old estimate of Dr. Ernst Engel, the head of the Prussian bureau of statistics, that the cost of bringing up a child in Germany was $30.00 a year for the first five years, $37.50 a year for the second five years, and $45.00 a year for the third five years, making a total of $562.50 as the cost of bringing up a child to the age of fifteen, when it is presumably able to support itself. Kapp said that it would cost at least double that to bring up a child in the United States, so that the value of each immigrant above the age of fifteen is from $1000 to $1200. On this basis the money value of the immigration each year is very large. In the year 1886, for instance, the number of immigrants above the age of

---

[1] Kapp, Immigration and the New York Commissioners, etc., p 146.

fifteen was 263,189. Taking them at the German valuation they represent a sum equal to nearly $150,000,000, or at the American valuation a sum nearly twice that. The immigration of 1886 was not excessive, — in fact it was below what it is now, so that immigration represents hundreds of millions of dollars saved to the United States each year.

It is easy to point out how superficial this method of estimate is. As Rümelin says,[1] it belongs to the half-truths or pseudo-truths of political economy. The worth of a man is not measured by the cost of bringing him up, coupled with the consideration whether he has paid this cost back to the community. If that were true, a man's greatest worth would be when he first acquires physical strength; and the experienced man of forty would be of less value than the raw youth of eighteen. Nor is every man worth the cost of his bringing up. Of the immigrants into this country, some are already disabled, some will die in a few years, others will land in the poor-house, and still others will be found in our asylums and gaols, an absolute burden to the community to which they are said to be worth a thousand dollars each. The value of a man lies in his capacity and character, not in what it has cost to bring him up. If the immigrant finds an opportunity to exercise the talents

---

[1] Rümelin, Bevölkerungslehre, in Schönberg's Handbuch der Politischen Oekonomie, 2 Ausg. Bd. 2, S. 916.

he possesses, he is of value to himself and to the community whether he has cost $500 or $1000 to bring to the age of manhood. If he is a vagabond, ignorant, lazy, or vicious, then he is worse than of no value to the community that receives him, and the country that has gotten rid of him may well be congratulated upon losing that form of capital.

This way of looking upon the cost of bringing up children as an investment of capital is wholly fallacious. The cost of rearing children can scarcely be said to be a loss of capital. It is true that they have cost the parents labor and sacrifice; but the sacrifice has been made and the parents are in the same position in which they would otherwise have been, save that they have worked harder and have not had so many enjoyments as they might have had. They have preferred to bring up the children instead. So also Kapp's statement that it costs double to bring up a child in this country compared with the cost of bringing it up in Germany is in one sense true, but in another sense it shows the fallacy of the whole estimate. The reason why it costs double in this country is because we are so well off that we spend more on our children. We are so well off that we can afford to have children and to bring them up in an expensive way. That is the reason why our ancestors had such large families in the early days of the republic. Our forefathers were not wasting their capital, neither were they making an investment of capital; they were simply marrying and having large families because they were well-to-do. It is not to be looked upon as a matter of dollars and cents. It is a good thing, socially and morally, that men should have children and rear them. This forms the family tie and keeps up the continuity of social habits and traditions. If we could take our children at birth and send them over to Europe and have them brought up as German peasants or Irish cottiers or Italian lazzaroni at little or no expense,— would it pay us to do it?

A second method of estimating the economic value of the immigrant is to say that he should be valued in the same way as a slave. Whatever may be the character of the immigrants,— it is argued,— whether they come from the upper or the lower classes of society, whether they are desirable additions to the political and social elements in our country or not, whether they are ignorant or intelligent, skilled or unskilled,— they do represent a certain amount of brute force. There are a certain number of able-bodied laborers landed on our shores and prepared to do the rough work which we have to do. They certainly possess the value of the slave who was also ignorant, unskilled and often degraded. The value of a slave before the war was perhaps $800 or $1000. Every able-bodied immigrant is worth at least that, and may be worth more if he is a skilled laborer.

The fallacy is very similar to that exposed above, — namely, that of looking upon the man as an investment of capital. The slave *is* an investment of capital. He can be made to do a certain amount of unskilled labor by fear of the lash. He can be fed and clothed in the cheapest possible way, so as to make the net return from his labor as great as possible. If he is not profitable in one employment he can be turned into another, and if he ceases to be of value in one part of the country he can be sold into another part. As a last resort, if it does not pay to support him, he can be worked to death and his place taken by new purchases or importations — as was said to be the policy at one time of the sugar planters in the West Indies, who found it more profitable to work their slaves hard for a few years and then import new ones, than to keep those they had in good condition.

But the immigrant is no slave. He is a free man. He works or not as he pleases, and when and where he pleases or chance determines. His consumption is regulated only by his own desires or his ability to satisfy those desires. It may be prudent and economical; it may be foolish, wasteful and even injurious. He may be willing to work; he may be entirely unwilling. The only lash is that of hunger, which in many individual cases proves utterly ineffective. The trouble is that it can be escaped by stealing or begging. To compare the value of the immigrant with that of a slave is to say that the free negroes of the West Indies are of the same economic value now that they were when they were slaves; while the fact is that liberty has simply taught them not to labor.[1]

There is, now, a third method of estimating the economic value of the immigrant, which is scientifically correct and which is the only one to be employed if we are determined to express in figures the value of this increase of our labor force. The value of the immigrant depends upon the amount of wealth he will add to the community before he dies. From this of course must be deducted the cost of maintaining him while he lives. The result will be his net earnings. This, capitalized at the current rate of interest, gives us the present value of the man. It is exactly on the principle of a life annuity. To calculate the value of an immigrant you must know his expectation of life, his earning capacity and his expenses or the cost of maintaining him. The method is not easy of application, for we do not possess these data. But the method is not at all a new one and

[1] See Mr. Froude's doleful account of the condition of the blacks in the West Indies.

some applications of it will throw light on our problem.

Dr. William Farr, for so many years the head of the statistical department of the registrar general's office in England, in a paper read before the London statistical society in 1853 [1] gave elaborate tables showing the present value of the future earnings of an agricultural laborer, his future cost of maintenance, and the value of the excess, which is the economic value of the man. Thus, at the age of twenty, the value of an agricultural laborer's future wages is £482; the value of the necessary cost of future maintenance is £248; and the net value of his services is therefore £234. Or, taking the whole of the male agricultural laborers into account their mean gross value was £349; the mean gross value of the subsistence of the laborer as child and man was £199, leaving £150 as the net value of agricultural laborers, or of the whole male population estimated by this standard of the agricultural laborer. To extend the calculation to the whole population, including females, the standard might be lowered from £150 to £110. In the thirty-ninth report of the registrar general (1877) Dr. Farr proceeds to make an application of this method to the question of the loss to England by emigration. He says: [2]

[1] William Farr, Vital Statistics, p. 60.
[2] Ibid.

"The emigrants are chiefly adults married and unmarried; the men greatly exceeding the women in number. A few infants accompany their parents. Valuing the emigrants as the agricultural laborers have been valued at home — taking age and service into account — the value of the emigrants in 1876 was £175 per head.

"If we may venture to apply this standard to the whole period it will follow that the money value of the 8,000,000 people that left England, Scotland, and Ireland in the years 1837-1876 was 1400 million pounds sterling or on an average about £35,000,000 a year."

This valuation, $875 per capita, is certainly high enough to satisfy the most ardent advocate of immigration.

Recently Dr. Becker,[1] the head of the German statistical office, has used the same method in estimating the value of the German emigrant. Wages are lower and the margin of living is much closer in Germany than in England. In fact the author reckons that, taking the whole laboring population of Germany of the class from which the emigrants come, their future earnings just cover their future consumption. The emigrants, however, are a select class as to sex and age, and he reckons the present value of the emigrant at from 800 to 900 marks, that is, from $200 to $225.

This, Dr. Becker thinks, is a real loss to Germany.

[1] Becker, Unsere Verluste durch Wanderung, cited above.

Farr takes a more cheerful view of the effect on England. He says:

"It may be contended that emigration is a loss to the mother country. It seems so. It is like the export of precious goods for which there is no return. But experience proves that simultaneously with this emigration there has been a prodigious increase of the capital of the country, especially in recent years. Wages have risen and the value of the laborer has risen in proportion. . . . When the man leaves the village where he was born and bred, he leaves the market open to his fellows, he removes to a field where his work is in demand, and carries his fortune with him. It is the same way when he emigrates to the colonies. His parents in rearing him have expended their gains in the way most agreeable to themselves. They have on an average five children, instead of two or three, or none. Taking a wider view, the emigrants create articles of primary use with which in exchange they supply the mother country; they have sent to England in the thirty-nine years wheat, cotton, wool, gold to the value of hundreds of millions."[1]

But whatever the gain or loss to the home country, both authors are agreed that there is a gain to the new country and that this gain is measured in this way. In fact, as wages are so much higher in the United States and living not very much dearer, the present value of the laborer is higher here than it was at home.

There is the same fallacy in this estimate as in

---

[1] Fawcett, on the other hand, thought that state-aided emigration in connection with compulsory education caused a direct loss to the community. Political Economy, p. 602.

the other two. The present capitalized value of the laborer's future wages depends on his having an opportunity to earn those wages. The immigrant has an economic value only if there is opportunity for him to work. He is of use to us only if we can make him useful. This will depend on his character and capacity and on the work still to be done in this country and the number of men we have to do it. This brings us to the question: Do we need the immigrant? Here we have an immense labor force offered us. Can we make use of it? The answer to this question is difficult if not impossible. Some considerations of the following sort may be suggestive.

In order to form any opinion on the question, whether or not we can make use of the immigrants, it is necessary to know what they can do, that is, what their occupation or profession is; and, again, to know whether they settle in that part of our country where such occupation can be successfully pursued. I believe far too little attention has been paid to these two points. Immigration has been welcomed as so much addition to our labor force, or denounced as a burden to our poor rates, without considering whether it is of the right sort or in the right place. But that determines most often whether it is to be a gain or a burden.

It is not probable that our statistics of the occupations of immigrants are very accurate in detail.

They are collected in too hurried and careless a way to be strictly correct. But for our present purpose they are sufficient to show that the mass of the immigration is of common, unskilled labor.

The statistics collected by the United States show the following results: Nearly one-half of the immigrants are without occupation, this including of course the greater part of the women and children. Of the immigrants with occupations about 1 per cent. are professional, about 22 per cent are skilled artisans, and 76 per cent are unskilled laborers — for that is what the column "miscellaneous" in the statistics really amounts to. In other words three-fourths of the immigrants are unskilled laborers.

These statistics are confirmed by those from the other side of the water. In 1886, out of 54,507 adult males (twelve years of age and upward) of British and Irish origin, who migrated from Great Britain to the United States, 26,096 were general laborers, 9171 were agricultural laborers, gardeners, carters, etc., and 12,906 were of occupations not stated.[1] These latter were either boys or common laborers, so that it is entirely safe to say that three-fourths of the emigrants of British and Irish origin are laborers.

Of the emigrants from Germany in 1886 that came by the way of Hamburg, 33.58 per cent were returned

[1] Statistical Tables relating to Emigration and Immigration from and into the United Kingdom, 1887.

The Economic Gain by Immigration. 115

as of no occupation. These are presumably women and children. 24.89 per cent were laborers, 15.87 per cent were agriculturists, 16.70 per cent were of the industrial class and 8.96 per cent were of the commercial class. Excluding the persons without occupations, the laborers and agriculturists constituted 61 per cent of those emigrants having occupations.[1]

Of the emigrants from Italy in 1885 (fourteen years of age and upward), 59.63 per cent were husbandmen and shepherds, 12.43 per cent were navvies, porters, and other day laborers, 13.30 per cent were artisans and operatives, and 5.49 per cent were masons and stone cutters. That is, more than 72 per cent were farmers or laborers.[2]

It appears, then, that three-fourths of our immigrants are agriculturists or common laborers. Can we make use of that kind of labor? One more analysis will be necessary before we answer that question. One of the greatest misconceptions about this whole subject is, I believe, that all we have to do with this mass of immigrants is to put them on the land "out West" and make farmers of them; and farming is commonly conceived of as an unskilled occupation. Now the great mass of these laborers are not farmers at all or even farm laborers, as will

[1] Bulletin de l'Institut international de statistique, 1887, 2ème livraison, p. 53.
[2] Statistica della emigrazione italiana per gli anni 1884 e 1885, p. xix.

be seen by reference to the statistics of Great Britain and Germany above. In the statistics of the United States, also, the farmers are always outnumbered by the laborers pure and simple. Thus in 1886 there were returned 20,600 farmers and 86,853 laborers. Even of these so-called farmers it is to be remarked that they are not farmers in our sense of the word. They are the farm laborers accustomed to do the rough hand work on the farms of Europe. They do not possess either the skill, or the capital, or the knowledge of modern methods and the use of agricultural machinery, requisite to enter into the ranks of the farmers of this country. At best they can only drift on to the farms and become farm laborers, and perhaps after a while, by thrift and industry, start kitchen gardening in the neighborhood of a large city. However, these farmers and farm laborers can be easily disposed of. There is plenty of land in this country, and if they will really become farmers or farm laborers there will be no trouble in providing them places and opportunity to earn a living. But the great mass of laborers are not farmers and are not fitted to become farmers. If you put them on the land they would not know how to cultivate it. Of their own disposition they are less likely to go into farming than anything else, because a farmer must rely to a great extent upon himself. This self-reliance is the quality they possess least of all. The number of immigrants of this class is very large and it is this class that increases most with every increase of immigration. How numerous they are will be seen by the following figures:

NUMBER OF IMMIGRANTS CLASSED AS LABORERS, 1880–1888.

1880 105,012	1885 83,068
1881 147,816	1886 86,853
1882 209,605	1887 140,938
1883 136,071	1888 170,273
1884 106,478	Total (nine years) 1,186,114

These are the men who build our railroads, who clean our streets, who handle our freight, who are employed more or less in every factory for lifting and moving heavy weights, trucking, cleaning up, etc. Can we make use of these men and in this number? He would be a bold man who would assert that the United States, with its miles of railroad building every year, with its canals and river transportation, with its constantly expanding factory system, with its use of machinery whereby unskilled labor can be more and more utilized, cannot furnish employment to this common labor. In one sense, the newer a country is the more of this unskilled labor it needs, because it has more of the primary work to do — reclaiming the soil and making channels of communication. No one can look upon a map of the United States and see the immense unreclaimed territory, without saying to himself: There is room here for the unskilled labor of the world in reclaiming these deserts, in draining these swamps, in opening up these distant regions. In the face of this generalization I shall only venture the following practical suggestions.

In every country this unskilled labor is of itself the most abundant. It constitutes the mass of the community. In it is found that great number of men who earn their daily bread literally by the sweat of their brow. In it are found all those who are not particularly intelligent and who, either from lack of inclination or want of opportunity, have not been trained to any great skill. They are the hewers of wood and the drawers of water, who form the lowest but necessary stratum of every society. I venture to assert, not only that they are present in every community in sufficient number, but that no community has ever found it difficult to produce them. What is difficult to produce is the intelligent and skilled workman, — the man who can take the initiative himself, who not only does work but makes work. Possibly fifty years ago we needed more of this common labor than we could produce ourselves; but we are not in that early civilization now. We have been receiving, too, an immense quantity of this kind of labor during these years. Ever since the great movement of 1846 the immigration has been predominantly of this character. We have in our employ hundreds of thousands of these unskilled laborers and their descendants.

I would suggest, again, that the progress of our civilization renders the demand for this unskilled labor less than it formerly was. We have not built all our railroads, but the country is fairly well opened. We have not brought all our land under cultivation, but we have taken up the better part of it, and there is no reason why we should desire to cultivate that inferior part which will make a less return for the labor. The first work of the pioneer has been done and will never have to be repeated. Then, again, the progress of civilization has enabled us to apply machinery to much of this work. The steam drill, the dredge, the derrick, do the work which was formerly done by men. We accomplish more with a few men than our ancestors did with hundreds. Steam takes the place of human muscle, and it is just as well that it is so. There is no advantage in our growing into the condition of those countries where it does not pay to use machinery because labor is so cheap. Let us seek increased cheapness not by making our labor cheap, but by inventions which shall make our labor effective.

Finally, I would suggest that to make this unskilled labor effective there ought to be some guarantee that it shall get to the place where it is needed, not merely stay where it happens to land. One would say that the place for this mere muscular labor is on the frontier, where it can do the rough work required. There is absolutely no guarantee that it will get there. The census of 1880 showed an immense preponderance of the foreign born in the cities, as did the census of Massachusetts for 1885. The truth about these unskilled laborers is, as every one knows, that they are in many cases stranded in the large cities where they form the nucleus for an ignorant, often depraved proletariat, living from hand to mouth, a burden to the poor rates and a social incubus on the community. This unskilled labor is not in its right place, the place where it aids the development of the country, but is in directly the wrong place, adding to the complexities of that already complex problem, the government of large cities.

The object of this long and minute consideration of the economic value of the immigrant is to point out that this is a question which cannot be settled off-hand by a simple affirmative or negative. Our civilization is becoming so complex that we have to pay greater attention to the working of social forces than we have in times past. It is now a serious matter if we get too much labor or labor of the wrong kind. We, like the countries of the old world, have our periodical commercial crises and our host of unemployed. The Commissioner of Labor reported in 1886 that according to his estimate there were a million men unemployed in the United States, and that the underconsumption caused by their inability to buy was enough to account in large measure at least for the continued commercial depression. The Massachusetts Bureau of Labor Statistics said in its report for 1887: "that out of a total of 816,470 persons employed in gainful occupations in that state, 241,589, or 29.59 per cent were unemployed at their principal occupation, on an average, 4.11 months during the year; in short that about one-third of the total persons engaged in remunerative labor were unemployed at their principal occupation for about one-third of the working time."

In the face of these facts it is no longer possible to say that there is such a demand for labor in this country that immigration will take care of itself. I do not mean to assert that there is absolutely no more room for additional labor force. But I do say that we need not concern ourselves lest we should not have labor force enough; while there is rather reason to apprehend that continued additions from outside sources may increase the supply of laborers faster than the opportunities for work.

It was one of the theories of Karl Marx that the modern industrial system creates a sort of reserve army of proletariat. When times are good, all the men are employed. As soon as times are bad, the employer discharges a portion of his men and they are thrown into the street to look out for themselves. Some of them die; others are weakened by disease and hardship so that they are never able-bodied workmen again; some fall on the poor relief; others are added to the ranks of the criminal and the vicious. It is absolutely necessary for the modern factory system that there should be this reserve army in order that it may take advantage of the times of increased demand. But it creates a proletariat which is a burden to the community at large. It is a serious question whether we are not creating such a proletariat at the present time.

CHAPTER VII.

COMPETITION WITH AMERICAN LABOR.

ALL the arguments regarding the economic gain to this country through free immigration proceed from the standpoint of the production of wealth. They ignore the character and social influence of the immigrant, and content themselves with showing the advantage of having command of this increased labor force which is furnished us free of charge by the nations of Europe. Too often, also, they pass over a second question which even from the purely economic standpoint deserves consideration. That is as follows: What effect has this constant immigration on the labor already here? on its wages, its standard of living and its contentment? This question is no less important than the preceding one,— in fact in many respects it is more important. For the first is merely a question of more or less rapid growth in material wealth, which, in the present condition of the United States, is a matter of minor importance. But the second ramifies out into the great question of the condition of the working classes, of their content or discontent, and this at the present time is the most serious problem confronting civilized nations. We have not vindicated free immigration even economically, when we have shown that it increases the production of wealth. We must go one step further and determine its effect on the laboring class of America.

Complaints in regard to this have not been wanting. These complaints will be found to be of three kinds. In the first place, it is asserted that the addition of a thousand men a day to the number of laborers in this country tends to lower wages and throw men out of employment. Coupled with this is the notion that if the national government protects the American workman against foreign competition in products, it should protect him equally against direct competition of alien labor. A second complaint is of the importation of laborers under contract for the express purpose of taking the places of men already employed, which renders nugatory all the efforts of labor organizations to increase wages by strikes or combinations. And, in the third place, it is said that many of the immigrants have a lower standard of living than is customary in America so that competition with them on a plane of decent living is impossible. It will be found on examination that these three questions are entirely distinct in character; the first is almost purely an economic question, while the last two are largely social.

It is difficult to measure the direct competition which immigration brings on the working men of America. It is undoubtedly considerable. It may, indeed, be said that our industries are constantly expanding and by this expansion are able to absorb an additional number of laborers without injuring the former ones. This additional labor force may even be necessary to give that remunerative employment to capital which after all is the source of the prosperity of the entire community, laboring men included. There is nothing more discouraging to enterprise than a scarcity of labor, or labor at such high prices or so completely under the control of labor unions that no calculations can be made for the future and no contracts undertaken with the certainty that they can be filled at the agreed price. An expansive prosperity is more conducive to abundance than a narrow-minded conservation of individual interests. And working men, by monopolizing the opportunity to work, may destroy it.

Direct competition in the case of skilled labor would not seem to be very severe. As we have seen in the previous chapter only about ten per cent of the immigrants are skilled laborers. In 1886 the only classes of which the number was over 1,000 were as follows. Bakers, 1,209; blacksmiths, 1,420; butchers, 1,190; carpenters and joiners, 3,678; clerks, 3,027; mariners, 1,803; masons, 1,835; mechanics,

1,886; miners, 3,469; shoemakers, 1,681; tailors, 2,682; tobacco manufacturers, 1,160. Certainly the competition brought about by the annual addition of that number of men to each trade cannot be very great.

But this is looking only at the surface of things. When we remember that over thirty per cent of the persons engaged in manufacturing, mechanical and mining industries in the United States are of foreign birth, it is clear that either the statistics of immigration are grossly inaccurate or that large numbers of the immigrants learn a trade after they arrive here. The latter is probably the case. The truth is that the introduction of machinery has made many occupations which were once skilled, really unskilled, or such as can be learned after a short apprenticeship. The unskilled foreign labor readily masters the simple operations of the machine and then crowds into the factories and workshops. It is here that the unskilled and "miscellaneous" categories in the statistics of immigration find their resting place. The lower classes of Europe crowd into the factories of America, driving out labor that was intelligent if not actually skilled. As has often been said, the Irish drove the New England girls out of the cotton factories of Massachusetts, and now the French Canadians are driving out the Irish.

It is here that the American or Americanized

laborer is being subjected to the most strenuous competition. This labor from Europe is not inaptly labelled "miscellaneous" by the bureau of statistics. It comes ready to take up any occupation in which it can earn a living. I do not suppose that the French Canadians when they come to the United States enter themselves as cotton-mill operatives. Probably they have never seen a cotton-mill in their life. They are only potentially cotton-mill operatives; but they fill up the mills just the same. So very likely the Hungarians who are imported to dig coal in the Hocking Valley are not miners when they arrive. They take the place of the former workmen, however, just as if they were *bona fide* miners.

It is sometimes argued that this lower labor simply displaces the former by shoving it up to a higher position, and thus benefits not only itself but also the former. It is said that the American girl no longer needs to work in the factory because that kind of labor is now performed by the Irish or the French Canadian, and the American is left free for higher kinds of occupation. If that were universally true it would be a favorable process. But we have no guarantee that it works in that way. It may and it may not. Where the immigration is large in amount the displacement may occur without any corresponding "placement," so to speak, elsewhere.

Or it may force the displaced labor to another locality and change the character of the whole community, and very probably for the worse. Relations will certainly adjust themselves in the end, but it is optimistic fatalism to say that they will always adjust themselves for the better.[1]

Again the relation between free immigration and a protective tariff does not appear altogether clear. Protectionists commonly say the tariff is for the protection of American against the poorer-paid labor of Europe. But what avails it to keep out the goods and introduce the laborer and put him side by side with the American in the competition for producing goods at a low price? For the manufacturer it is obviously an advantage to have a monopoly of the market for his goods and a free command of the market in which to buy labor. But the advantage to the working man is not obvious. Notwithstanding this the protectionists are commonly in favor of unrestricted immigration.

The reverse position of free trade in goods and restriction of immigration seems to me much more consistent. It is sometimes said that it is of no use to keep out the laborer if at the same time you admit

[1] The testimony before the House of Commons Committee on Immigration is very instructive on this point. In three trades, tailoring, boot and shoe-making, and cabinet-making immigration seems simply to have produced an over-supply of labor and given rise to the "sweating system." See *post*, p. 136.

the commodities in which his labor is embodied. But there is this difference. If you admit the goods you pay for them in others made by our laborers with all the advantages of our natural resources, improved machinery, superior organization of labor, etc. But if you admit the foreign laborer you set him down side by side with the American, furnished with all the advantages which the latter possesses, and in direct competition with him. In the former case you get the advantage of his low wages and cheap living by trading your superior advantages against them. In the latter you divide your advantages with him, and then compete for the same market. But whatever position one may take in regard to free trade in goods, it is unreasonable to say that you are protecting the American laborer when you admit free trade in labor.

The competition is felt more keenly when the laborers are imported under contract. There have been a large number of such cases during the last ten years. Many of the Italians who have worked on our railroads have been brought by contractors for that purpose. The New York commissioner of labor in 1885 found a contractor in Buffalo who admitted that he had furnished four hundred foreigners to railroad companies and other corporations during the preceding year. We hear of similar cases in New Jersey, Kansas, Iowa and Wisconsin. The commissioner of the labor bureau in the last named state asserts that in the year 1886 the state was flooded with circulars from an Italian Labor and Construction company in New York offering to let men "for tunnelling, grading, mining, breaking stone, laying ties, repairing washouts, laying water and gas mains, street cleaning, shovelling snow," or to take such work as sub-contractors "at figures that will repay inquiry." "Contractors will find that the authority of this company over the men it furnishes is of special advantage in all dealings it may have with them." It is notorious that the mine owners in Pennsylvania and Ohio have imported laborers to take the places of men at work in the mines.

In New England, French Canadians are brought in to work in the cotton-mills and at brick laying. At the latter trade they work during the summer and return to Canada for the winter. In New York the labor commissioner reported similar cases of masons who were brought over here during the busy season and returned to Europe in the winter.

The testimony before the Ford immigration committee brought to light several cases of the importation of laborers under contract in spite of the law of 1885 against it. That law is extremely difficult to enforce because it is almost impossible to get evidence. The laborer is interested in concealing the fact, and there is no mark by which the inspectors at Castle Garden can tell that he is under contract.[1]

Working men protest against the importation of labor under contract not on account of the small amount of additional competition involved in it, but because it destroys the efficacy of their labor organizations. It renders strikes harmless, and the demand for increased wages or the protest against reduction of wages equally unavailing. It makes the employer master of the situation, for the supply of this imported labor is practically unlimited.

Competition is rendered more difficult for the American laborer and more disastrous for the community because many of the immigrants of recent years represent a very low standard of living. The reason these imported laborers can displace the American by taking lower wages is that they live in a way which it is impossible for the native workman to imitate and which it would be a misfortune for the civilization of the community if he should. It is

---

[1] The evidence was in regard to Swedes brought over to take the place of strikers at Fall River, p. 111; Hungarian and Italian miners in Pennsylvania, p. 205, ff.; miners in the Hocking Valley, Reports of consuls, p. 74; Bohemians and Russian Jews as cigar makers, p. 364, and p. 379; cotton-mill operatives in Newark, p. 370 and p. 450; watch case makers, p. 425; stone cutters employed on the capitol, Austin, Texas, p. 138; worsted mill hands at Forge Village, p. 578; ship carpenters in Detroit, p. 624. Much of the testimony was very indefinite, but some written contracts were presented.

not merely that the immigrants have received less wages and are less well off in the old country than in this. That would be true of the mass of them since the movement began, and the very fact that they expected better wages in this country has in many cases been the chief inducement to come. But in former times most of them had the desire for a higher style of living and quickly lifted themselves up to the American standard. In recent years, however, a class has come, accustomed to a distinctly lower standard, with no notion of anything else, perfectly content to live as at home, and whose only ambition has been to save enough to return to the old country.

The types of this class of people with which we have become familiar during the last few years are the Italians, the French Canadians, the Poles and the Hungarians. The causes which have contributed to their immigration are the cheapness of transportation, the solicitation of steamship agents and the importation of contract labor.

It is scarcely necessary to describe the standard of living of these people. Attention has been directed to it by newspapers, bureaux of labor statistics, labor organizations and the Congressional committee already mentioned. Italians testified before this committee that they were accustomed to live at home on fifteen cents a day. The committee visited in person the tenement houses in New York city, where these new comers lodge, and saw sights that almost baffle description. Huddled together in miserable apartments, in filth and rags, without the slightest regard to decency or health, they present a picture of squalid existence degrading to any civilization and a menace to the health of the whole community. Ignorant, criminal and vicious, eating food that we would not give to dogs, their very stolidity and patience under such conditions show that they lack the faintest appreciation of what civilization means.

Neither is it merely in the slums of great cities that we find this condition of things. In Connecticut the commissioner of the bureau of labor statistics speaks of the Italians in the following way:—

"The Italian immigrants come almost entirely from the southern districts of Italy. They come in rudely organized bodies, not as a rule under contract from the employers themselves, but under the leadership of certain of their own nation, who arrange concerning their employment and pay. The Italian's object in coming to this country is simple. He wishes to stay here until he can save two or three hundred dollars, and then go home again. This sum amounts to a competence in his own country, and enables him to pass the remainder of his days as a man of wealth and established position. . . .

"The task which he has before him is not a difficult one. . . . His expenses he is able to reduce to a minimum. In matters of personal comfort he is the reverse of exacting. He can bear an infinite amount of crowding, without apparently interfering with his enjoyment of life or sense of decency. His diet is simple; it is even cheaper than that of the French Canadian. While the Canadian relies largely on peas and other cheap and nutritious vegetables, the food of the Italian consists largely of stale bread, stale fruit and stale beer. The Italians use these things at a point where they cease to be marketable. Of fruit in particular, they save large quantities at a point where it has almost no commercial value, applying a kind of drying process of their own, and afterwards cooking the dried fruit from time to time as it is wanted."[1]

The Hungarians, Poles and Russians represent the same condition of things, as is proven by abundant testimony both in this country and before the British commission charged with the investigation of the immigration of foreigners. It is not the immigration of individual paupers and indigent persons that we have to do with, but the beginning of an influx of whole classes, that threatens to lower our

---

[1] Report, 1885, pp. 60 ff.

The Italians do not seem to be favorites anywhere. The consul of the United States at Marseilles, France, writes: "There are in this city more than 54,000 Italians, who hold toward the native laboring classes a relation somewhat similar to that of the Chinese in the Western American states. The Italian laborer is quite as industrious and even more economical than the Frenchman. His wants are so few and simple that he can exist upon a small percentage of his earnings, and in a competition of wages he underbids the native laborer. In several parts of this district there have been heard recently sharp protests, attended in some instances by violence, against the Piedmontese, who swarm across the frontier and seek employment in mines and tanneries and upon public works; but these manifestations have been promptly suppressed and denounced as uncivilized and dangerous to French working-people in other countries." Consular Reports, p. 71.

standard of material civilization. Suppose we raise up those who come to something like the level of the American laborer so that they will demand the same decencies and comforts of life and refuse to accept anything else; — there is an inexhaustible supply behind and new quotas will be brought over for the same purpose as before, namely, in order to obtain cheap labor.

In fact at our very doors we are trying an experiment of the sort, that is, to bring up a foreign community to our standard of living. The French Canadians are of the same class as the Italians, and for some years they have been flowing into New England. They work for less wages and live on cheaper food than the native American or the Irishman. They are steadily driving the natives out of the factory towns of New England. But they do not take the place of the old inhabitant in the social life of the community. They remain under the power of the priest; they economize in every way so as to return home; they do not send their children to the public schools; they add to the illiteracy if not to the vice and the crime of the community; they lower distinctly the general intelligence and civilization. There is an inexhaustible supply of them. When a mill owner wants additional laborers, he simply goes among those who are already here and asks them if they have any friends or relatives in the Dominion who would like to get employment. They all do know of such cases. The only difficulty is that they have not the means of coming. The agent advances the funds, the new men come and a fresh addition is made to the population, lacking every characteristic of value to the commonwealth except industry and a peaceable disposition.

One result of this kind of immigration will be the introduction of those abuses incident to the factory system, against which we have for so many years been battling with our factory and sanitary and school legislation. The testimony before the Ford committee [1] showed that the "sweating system" was already introduced in New York, with its miserable wages, long hours of work, employment of women and children, and disregard of all the decencies and health requirements of life. The testimony before the English committee on the immigration of foreigners into London was still more emphatic. Two or three trades, tailoring, boot and shoe-making, and cabinet-making have gone over into the hands of foreigners, mostly poor Russian and Polish Jews. The universal testimony was that these new arrivals, entirely destitute, ignorant of the language and accustomed to a low style of living, fell into the hands of the "sweater" almost as soon as they landed. The "sweater" is simply a sub-contractor who takes

[1] p. 222.

clothing or shoes, already cut, from the manufacturer, agreeing to do the necessary work on them for a given price per piece. There is great competition among these middle men and their number is always large because but little capital is required and it is easy to start in the business. The "sweater" then takes the bundle of clothes or shoes home to be made up. In a small room — sometimes a living room, sometimes a shop built out over a yard — he employs a number of men to assist him. Crowded together in this room, the atmosphere made foul by gas, by the coke fire used in heating the pressing irons and by human breath and exhalations, the men sit and work fourteen, sixteen and sometimes eighteen hours a day. The sweater retains one-half the sum received for the work, distributing the remainder among the workmen. The tendency is to reduce the earnings to the lowest possible point. The men are helpless. It is either work or starve. The labor is of such poor quality that a "greener" can learn the trade in a month's time, and if a man leave his place, it is immediately taken by an immigrant. The same competition reduces the wages of sewing women to the merest pittance, and the testimony showed that women in London were working fourteen hours a day in order to earn a shilling. In New York it was also shown that the wages of sewing women had been reduced by the competition of Russian and Polish men who would work for less wages.

It is this kind of competition that is unfair to our working classes and a danger to the community. It is unfair to ask the working man to compete against labor based on a standard of living which we should be unwilling to see him adopt. It is unwise of the community to allow a competition which, if unchecked, must bring the whole laboring class to a lower standard of civilization.

Most economists and statesmen now acknowledge that competition in the labor market should take place only on a certain plane of living. We have not allowed employers to drive any bargain they pleased with their employees. We have restricted the hours of labor for women and children; we have regulated the condition of the workshop and the factory; we have compelled the children to go to school. In other words we have had an eye to the maintenance of the standard of civilization for the present and the future. In so doing we have pursued not only a humanitarian but a sound political and economic policy, for it is not for the good of the community that any class should lose its position in civilization.

Such are the chief considerations in regard to the effect of immigration on the economic condition of the working classes in this country. It is not easy to measure the exact influence on wages. The chief effect is that the laborer is subject to a constant stress of competition which it is difficult for him to meet. All the old barriers of custom, nationality, and skill have been broken down and he is at the mercy of the market. Part of this is the natural result of the factory system of production, but a good deal is the effect of the constant supply of new and competing labor from abroad. No one employs the American because he is a man, or a neighbor, or a compatriot, but simply because he will take the least wages. The national pride in him and his work has ceased.

It has for a long time been a dogma of economists that labor suffers from its immobility. It is unable to transfer itself readily from one employment to another or from one place to another in order to get higher wages.[1] Cairnes said that competition affected wages only within certain groups. Where an occupation requires skill, it is impossible for others to enter it. It is true that the new generation may be trained into it, if it does not require too long an apprenticeship, and thus competition be introduced, but this process is difficult and very gradual. So

---

[1] Walker in The Wages Question (1876), p. 180, said: "We may fairly say that the laboring population is never likely to be more completely mobilized by intelligence and the possession of property than is desirable in order to render it certain that just the amount of movement from industry to industry, and from place to place, which may be required, will be effected."

Fawcett delighted to point out that agricultural wages were considerably lower in one English county than in another only a few miles distant, owing to the inertia of the agricultural laborer. Professor J. B. Clark has however demonstrated that the barriers between groups are steadily giving way owing to the spread of intelligence and education and the introduction of machinery, which does away with the skill formerly required. The immobility of labor in respect to place is being rapidly removed by the facilities for transportation and by immigration. When a strike occurs on the street railroads of New York city, unskilled labor flocks from all the neighboring cities to get the job. The Chicago, Burlington and Quincy railroad brought men from Pennsylvania, and in a few days it had duplicated its entire force of engineers and firemen. This mobility of labor is greatly assisted by the employers, who go so far as to import laborers from Europe in order to escape the demands of their men. In no country of the world has this barrier of distance and national prejudice been broken down so completely as in the United States. Our workmen are subject to competition from the world. Almost every strike at the present time ends in the defeat of the strikers.

For the working men of this country, with their high wages and high standard of living, it is a misfortune to have these barriers of distance, of acquired skill and of nationality fall away so completely. It renders their position one of great instability and uncertainty. It makes it impossible that they should calculate or provide for their future or that of their children. It destroys local attachments and settled feelings. It renders efforts to better their condition either by organization or by thrift and prudence almost entirely futile. Competition among laborers there will always be; and it is not desirable that they should be entire masters of the situation, for absolute power is no safer in their hands than in those of any other class of the community. But with the present mobility of labor described above, the competition from the laborers already in this country will be sufficient to secure us from any monopoly of labor.

It is well here to consider the true office of competition. Its object is simply to put a spur on producers so that they may be compelled to produce and sell as cheaply as possible. Monopoly is always dangerous because it acts as a shield to laziness, carelessness, and lack of enterprise, as well as gives the opportunity to charge extortionate prices. When a man has a monopoly, his profits are secure whether he makes the best use of his raw material, his capital and his labor, or not. When he is subject to competition all this is changed. He is obliged to stop the waste of material, to turn over his capital quickly, and undersold by his rival and soon swept into bankruptcy.

Normal competition is for the benefit of the community at large. The price of commodities is reduced to a point near the lowest possible cost of production. The productive forces of the community are utilized to the highest degree. The control of the processes of production comes into the hands of the most efficient masters. The direction of the labor force of the community is confided to the most skilful leaders. The incompetent, the vacillating, the stupid employer is forced out of the ranks, and his place is taken by the better man. This is the glory of the modern system of free competition, and it is to this system that we owe the immense strides made during the last hundred years in the production of wealth.

The laborer has shared in the blessings of free competition. The cheapening of articles of ordinary consumption has come to his benefit, for he is the largest aggregate consumer. Cheapness has led to increased demand for commodities and thus to greater demand for his services. The competent, enterprising employer can make labor more efficient and can thus pay higher wages; or, at least, wages go further owing to the cheapness of commodities. The condition of the laborer tends constantly to improve. He is in the favorable position of a man who is selling his products in a rising market and buying his supplies in a falling. His very expenditures (which increase as his position becomes more favorable, so that what was once consumed by the few is now the daily consumption of the many) make trade prosperous and employment greater. Here is a circle which is the reverse of vicious. Increased cheapness caused by industry, skill and inventiveness is a blessing to the whole community.

Suppose, however, that increased cheapness is gained by the substitution of labor with a lower standard of living;—the charmed circle is at once broken. The older labor never reaps the benefit of the increased cheapness. The laborers either lose their places and are thrown into the street, or are compelled to accept wages which will not give them the necessaries and comforts of life according to their standard. There is created a class of discontented and unambitious workmen, who are no longer interested in the prosperity of the community. Still further, from a purely economic point of view, there is no gain to the community at large. The degraded labor with its lower standard of living does not make the same demand for commodities that the old did; and the increased cheapness instead of bringing increased demand is accompanied by a decreased power of consumption. Even the employers, in the distressing competition caused by decreasing consumption, soon find that their profits have been reduced to the old level or even lower.

Two remarkable cases of this sort of substitution of lower standard labor for higher have occurred in the United States and sufficient time has elapsed to perceive the effects. One is the influx of French Canadians into New England; the other is the settlement of Scandinavians in the Northwest. Both of these nationalities are extremely industrious, frugal and peaceable. They are by no means the worst class of immigrants that we receive. As Professor Hadley says of the French Canadians: "In economy of food . . . they teach us a lesson from which we might learn a good deal. The trouble is that their economy does not stop at a point where it would be desirable."[1] The Scandinavians have been the most powerful element in the development of several states in the West. But what is the result after we have acquired these new elements in our population? The following description is a newspaper account but is confirmed by other testimony.[2]

"They [the French Canadians] come in families, but never to remain more than a few years, or long enough to save two or three thousand dollars with which to purchase a Canadian estate big enough to support them all in affluence and genteel superiority over their neighbors. Then they go back. The accumula

[1] Connecticut Labor Bureau Report, 1885, p. 60.
[2] The (N. Y.) Evening Post, October 22, 1888.

tion of this fund is not a matter of much time either. The pay is small, it is true, but there is a ready explanation of their speedy acquisition of wealth. Where the native earned $12 a week, his Canadian successor gets $7, or at best $9, while the woman workers average as a rule from 75 to 90 cents per day, perhaps now and then $1. Those whom they replace received from $8 to $10 per week. Here then is the explanation. They all work. From the father and mother, daughters and sons, to the smallest boy in the family, they are employed at the picker, the loom, or in the mule loft gathering up empty bobbins from the long vibrating spinners. The fund thus acquired goes into the common purse for the common maintenance and for the common coming estate in Canada. Thus in a comparatively short period the sum is raised. While inborn frugality and the economy taught by bitter experience somewhat facilitates this, the true reason lies in the fact stated; it is a striking contrast, this utilization of every member of the *habitan* family, with the custom of the American, Irish, or German operative, who as a rule endeavors to support himself and his family on the product of his individual exertions.

"The undesirable effects of Canadian occupation are felt not alone in the great centres of industry. They have pushed out into the little villages, which in many cases mortgaged themselves to induce mill corporations to set up shop among them, that the townspeople might have employment, with increased population, increased valuation, and increased business. Such little hives of toil abound in plenty throughout Maine and Massachusetts — one or two mills making small hamlets bustling and prosperous. The blight of the French Canadian has now come over these, and he predominates among their working classes, destroying the social economy and lowering the general standing of the town."

In the same way another writer comments on the success of the Scandinavians in the West. They have succeeded where the American with a better start has failed. They have acquired farms and now live in a state of great comfort. In a certain sense it is a survival of the fittest. "But is it the survival of the fittest? Has the best man, the most valuable citizen, the man on whom the nation could depend in its hour of need, the man of brains, of energy and enterprise survived? Or has the man who could endure the hardest work and live on the coarsest fare driven the better man to the wall and survived because he was trained in a school of toil and direful poverty to a life which no American will endure if he can possibly escape its hard conditions?"[1]

What then has the community gained by the substitution of this cheaper labor force? The American labor is forced elsewhere, the standard of living of the laboring class is lowered, its consumptive power is decreased, and the civilization of the country is degraded. Such is the effect of unrestricted free competition without any regard to the plane on which the competition is conducted.

[1] Letter from Fargo, Dakota, in The New York Times, July 24, 1887.

CHAPTER VIII.

SOCIAL EFFECTS OF IMMIGRATION.

THE whole life of a nation is not covered by its politics and its economics. Social science is not composed simply of the science of government and political economy. Civilization does not consist merely of free political institutions and material prosperity. There is a realm outside of political and economic life which pertains to civilization and which is covered by what may be termed social science in its narrower sense. The morality of a community, its observance of law and order, its freedom from vice, its intelligence, its rate of mortality and morbidity, its thrift, cleanliness and freedom from a degrading pauperism, its observance of family ties and obligations, its humanitarian disposition and charity, and finally its social habits and ideals are just as much indices of its civilization as the trial by jury or a high rate of wages. These things are, in fact, the flower and fruit of civilization,—in them consists the successful "pursuit of happiness" which our ancestors coupled with life and liberty as the inalienable rights of a man worthy of the name.

Democracy and national wealth, the characteristics of the present century, are valuable as they contribute to these signs of prosperity and content and good-living.

Nothing, however, is more illusive than the attempt to gauge these characteristics of a nation's position in civilization. We can compare the constitutional and administrative systems of different countries and say which unites the greatest security for life and property with the greatest liberty of the individual. Statistics of trade, manufactures and wealth give some notion of the material prosperity of a nation. But there is no adequate expression for the degree of its morality, or even its respect for law, much less for the tone of its social life and the loftiness of its social ideals. It is for this reason that it is impossible to say of the different civilized nations of the world which is the most civilized. It is true that this is due to some extent to difference in standards, so that the Englishman will prize most highly that which is English and the German that which is German, because the measurements are necessarily subjective in each case; but if there were a common standard of measurement it would be impossible to apply it to such complex and delicate phenomena.

We are in the same position when we try to measure the social effects of immigration. The people of the United States started out at the beginning of this century with certain social traits and characteristics which doubtless would have endured or developed, modified more or less by the peculiar forces of our surroundings and external history. There can scarcely be a doubt, however, that this development has been further changed and modified by the addition of millions of persons of other races, from other civilizations, and with other ideals of social life. This modification may have been for good or it may have been for evil, — in either case it is almost impossible to trace it. Still further, many of these foreign elements have been here for a long period of time; they have become inextricably intermingled with the native elements so that they can no longer be disentangled; they have been modified by our institutions and environment so that they have become constituent parts of the whole. It would be absurd to trace effect back to a specific cause or to say that certain desirable things are the inheritance from our American ancestry and that others, — undesirable ones, — are the result of immigration.

We can, however, study tendencies. We can distinguish certain characteristics of the American people before the immigration commenced and say whether we are preserving or losing them. We have statistics of the participation of persons of foreign birth in the crime, vice and illiteracy of the community so that we can reason that the average is increased or decreased by their presence. All these things are tendencies only. They may be merely temporary evils which will cure themselves, and which should cause no uneasiness. We must not lay too much stress on figures alone, for they may be badly gathered or misleading in many respects. With this proviso we go on to study certain facts about the participation of our citizens of foreign birth in the social life of the community.

From general observation and from the statistics of occupations we know that the great mass of immigrants come from the lower classes, and it is always true that mortality is greater, and crime, vice, pauperism and illiteracy more prevalent among the lower classes than among the higher. It is only natural to expect therefore that the foreign born will contrast unfavorably with the native population in all these respects, simply because they represent more numerously these lower classes. It is not necessarily true that these people are more depraved or unfortunate than the corresponding class in our own country, but they simply appear so because we are comparing a lower class with a population including both the lower and the upper class. This does not change the fact, but it alters the complexion of the fact. It is not an indictment against the individual, for he may not be any more vicious or indigent than his position in society compels him to be;

but it is an indictment of the movement so to speak which forces into our population an abnormal proportion of the class that contributes to the crime, vice and pauperism of the community.

This distinction is an important one. For if criminality and poverty are simply the result of poor surroundings, there is a possibility that improved economic condition and higher social position may remove the tendency and change the immigrant into a virtuous, law-abiding and self-supporting citizen. In many cases there is not the slightest doubt that residence in the United States under the more favorable conditions has done this. Unfortunately our statistics cover only the first generation and these effects work themselves out most completely in the second and succeeding generations. It must always be borne in mind, therefore, that the statistics themselves are not a condemnation *in toto* of the persons to whom they pertain, but only indicate that they have come from unfortunate conditions and that the regenerative forces have not yet had a chance to work. When these forces have had a chance we may witness one of those wonderful transformations which almost make us believe, in social science, that a man's character is the product of his environment.

This distinction points to a further investigation that will be necessary. That is, whether there are any influences at work in Europe for the purpose of selecting and sending to us the depraved and weak. Such a process condemns itself at once. It deliberately chooses out of bad material that which is the worst and imposes it upon us. This is a process of natural selection which can only be a hardship to us and work us evil. All schemes of deportation of criminals and paupers, of state-assisted and charity-assisted emigration must be condemned and protested against by us. This is in reality the most important part of the present investigation and will require close treatment in the following chapter.

One more observation may be made here in regard to the statistics of vice and crime and their relation to the foreign born. Mortality, sickness, crime, vice, pauperism, insanity and most bodily afflictions become more frequent with advancing age. As we have already seen both immigrants and foreign born are abnormally represented in the middle and upper age classes. This is true of the immigrants because of the large number of adult males. It is still more true of the foreign born as contrasted with the native born, because the children of the former, born after the arrival in this country, are classed with the native born. The result is that any comparison of the amount of crime or vice or pauperism among the foreign born as compared with the native born is unfair. Owing to the advanced age of the former we should expect a greater amount. It is in most cases impossible to disentangle the statistics so as to correct this error. We can only make allowance for it.

There are no mortality statistics for the whole of the United States that are of any value and absolutely none that would show the difference in mortality between the native and the foreign born. It is said by Dr. Billings, who had charge of the vital statistics of the Tenth Census, that the mortality is greater among the foreign born than among the natives, just as it is greater among the colored than among the whites; but this is in all probability due to the economic condition of those classes. In certain specific diseases the Irish and Germans show a larger mortality than the native born; but any conclusions from the data are vitiated by the fact mentioned above that the children of the foreign born are numbered among the natives, so that it is impossible to attribute the increased mortality to race or nationality. It would be an extremely interesting and valuable inquiry to determine the influence of the foreign born on our birth and mortality rate and the prevalence of different diseases, but it needs much more accurate statistics than any we possess as yet.

Particular attention has been directed to the large proportion of insane in the United States who are of foreign birth. The census of 1880 returned 65,651 insane people as of native birth, and 26,346 as of foreign. That is the foreigners are nearly one in three of the insane, while they are only one in eight of the population. So Dr. Hoyt, the Secretary of the New York State Board of Health, says: "The number of insane committed to its (New York's) various state hospitals for acute cases during 1886, coming mainly from the rural counties, was 1248, of whom 868 were of native and 380 of foreign birth, it being an excess of nearly 42 per cent in the ratio of the insane in the foreign born population over the ratio of the insane arising from the native population." In the cities the proportion is much greater. These and similar figures have been subjected to a close analysis by Dr. C. L. Dana,[1] who points out that the proportion is not just, because insanity is a disease of adult life and the advanced age of the foreign born would naturally give them a large proportion. "The real facts are that about one-fifth of the persons susceptible to insanity are foreign born and these furnish a little over one-fourth of the insane, or a little over their just proportion. The ratio of foreign born insane to foreign born adults is .047 per cent and the ratio of native insane to native adult whites is .041 per cent, and to total native adults .036 per cent."

[1] Paper read before the American Social Science Association, September 7, 1887.

Dr. Dana has also studied the frequency of nervous diseases among the foreign and the native born. The conclusions of his valuable paper are as follows:

"1. The statements as to the excessive influence of immigrants in increasing nervous diseases are based on an incorrect study of statistics.

"2. The immigrants do slightly and directly increase the amount of insanity out of proportion to the native population.

"3. Immigration increases insanity indirectly through influence on social life and through introduction of poor nervous stock.

"4. Only a portion and certain special races have these tendencies to nervous and mental disease.

"5. The portion probably includes all Mongolians, the Asiatic and African Semites, Celts and Iberians.

"6. Immigrants develop a slight excess of organic nervous diseases, but fewer functional nervous diseases proportionally than the natives.

"7. Portions (the neuropathic races), however, soon develop functional diseases to excess in the children."

The census of 1880 showed an abnormal proportion of blind among the foreign born, but a small proportion of idiotic and of deaf and dumb, indicating clearly the influence of the age proportions.

It does not seem possible, however, with bald statistics to prove that the foreign born contribute more than their share to the defective and crippled portion of the community. Probably the most careful statistical investigation of this sort ever made in the

United States is that contained in the Massachusetts Census of 1885. The results there seemed to show that the foreign born contributed proportionally rather less than more to the defective classes.[1] The foreign born were 27.1 per cent of the whole population. Among the insane they were 37 per cent; among the chronic diseased they were 32.8 per cent; among the blind, 29.2 per cent; among the maimed, 27.8 per cent. In all these cases they were abnormally represented; but these are directly the cases where the defect is more frequent among adults than among children. But the foreign born were 34 per cent of the total population fourteen years of age and over, and 36.5 per cent of the population twenty years of age and over. It would seem therefore that they contributed rather less than their share to these defective classes. Still further while the foreign born were 27.1 per cent of the entire population, among the acute diseased they were only 26.3 per cent; among the lame, 25.5 per cent; among the bedridden, 22.8 per cent; among the paralytic, 21.5 per cent; among the deaf and dumb, 17 per cent; among the dumb, 16.4 per cent; among the deaf, 14.3 per cent; among the deformed, 14.4 per cent; and among the idiotic, 10.4 per cent. Some of these low percentages are explicable by the small number of children among the foreign born, just

---

[1] Massachusetts Census, 1885, vol. 1, part 2, p. cxxvii.

as the large percentages are by the large number of adults. Idiocy for instance is a disease of childhood and idiots are as a class short lived. The same is true to a less extent of the deaf and dumb and of the deformed. They are short lived because in most cases their infirmity is accompanied by a general constitutional weakness or by difficulty in gaining a livelihood. The bedridden and the paralytic again would probably be people well advanced in life and the foreign born are poorly represented in the highest age classes.

If we turn to other domains of social life, such as crime, pauperism, and illiteracy, we shall find the statistics much more unfavorable to the foreign born.

In regard to crime, it is an undoubted fact that a large proportion of our criminals and convicts are of foreign birth. This was shown by the census of 1880, although the statistics are so incomplete that they are scarcely worth quoting. The record of every prison and penitentiary in the United States would show an abnormal proportion of foreigners. I shall give only the statistics of Massachusetts, because they disclose not alone the place of birth of prisoners and convicts, but also their parent nativity. In Massachusetts in 1885 while 27.1 per cent of the population were foreign born, 40.60 per cent of the prisoners and 36.87 per cent of the convicts were foreign born. Even considering that 34 per cent of the population of the age of fourteen and over are foreign born, here is an abnormal proportion. But the figures are much more important when we take the parentage of the prisoners and convicts into consideration. Of the whole number of prisoners only 16.99 per cent have both parents native born, 60.30 per cent have both parents foreign born, while of the remainder the parentage was unknown. Of the convicts, 19.70 per cent have both parents native born, 51.14 per cent have both parents foreign born, and of the remainder the parentage is unknown. Even when we consider that 47.36 per cent of the people of Massachusetts were of foreign parentage, these proportions appear excessive.

It is in the statistics of pauperism and poor relief that we find the most accentuated indication of the presence of the immigrants. Many of them are almost entirely without resources. When they fail to get work their scanty savings are quickly exhausted and they are obliged to apply to public or private charity. The Secretary of State of New York reported in 1887 that there were in county poorhouses 9172 native paupers and 9288 foreign born paupers; while in city poorhouses there were 18,001 natives and 34,167 foreign born.

In Massachusetts they distinguish between homeless children and paupers. The former are less than twenty-one years of age and are dependants through no fault of their own. They have not had any real chance to support themselves. By far the greater number of them are of native birth as might be expected, viz., 93.25 per cent. But when we inquire as to the parentage of these children, we find that only 21.64 per cent of all the homeless children had both parents native born, that 31.29 per cent had both parents foreign born, and the remainder were of mixed or unknown parentage. It is the children of the immigrants who make up a large portion of this unfortunate class.

Of the paupers in Massachusetts 44.03 per cent are of foreign birth.[1] The parent nativity of the paupers is very doubtful; 26.23 per cent had both parents native born, 35.75 per cent had both parents foreign born, while the remainder were of mixed or unknown parentage.

The state of New York suffers more than any other from increased pauperism due to immigration, because the largest number of immigrants land at the port of New York, and if disabled or unable to work drift into the almshouse or asylum. The State Board of Charities gave the following facts in their annual report for the year 1887:

[1] It is an astonishing fact that out of 3696 paupers of foreign birth, 2829 were Irish, *i.e.* 76.5 per cent, although the Irish constituted only 46.4 per cent of the total foreign born. Massachusetts Census, vol. 1, part 2, p. 1265.

"During the year ending September 30, 1887, the Board, in pursuance of chapter 549 of the Laws of 1880, removed 216 chronic and disabled alien paupers to their homes in different countries of Europe as follows: To Germany, 68; to Ireland, 48; to England, 50; to Switzerland, 10; to Sweden, 9; to Norway, 8; to Scotland, 5; to Denmark, 1; to Austria-Hungary, 10; to France, 2; to Russia, 4; to Holland, 2; and to Italy, 2. All of these helpless persons were found in the poorhouses, almshouses and other charitable institutions of this state, most of whom had been dependent upon the state or its cities and counties from the time of their arrival in the country, and their physical and mental condition was generally such as to preclude their becoming self-supporting had they remained. From the records of the examinations of these persons, kept in the office of the Board, it appears that 153 of them reached this state through the port of New York, 34 through other United States ports, and 29 by the way of Canadian ports, all shipped from their homes abroad by the following agencies, viz.: By cities and towns, 36; by benevolent organizations and societies, 89; and by relatives and friends, 91. Their condition at the time of landing, as shown by the examinations, was as follows: Feeble-minded, so as to be incapable of providing for themselves, 52; imbecile, 26; lunatic, 25; vagrant and diseased, 27; crippled, 21; old and decrepit, 10; blind, 8; epileptic, 7; paralytic, 5; deaf and dumb, 3; otherwise infirm or diseased, 32. The total expense of removing these 216 helpless alien paupers to their respective homes abroad during the year was $4,358.47; the *per capita* expense, $20.18. The whole number of such paupers thus removed, since the act went into effect, has been 839; the aggregate expense, $18,000.37; the average expense per person, $21.45. The authorities of the cities and towns, and the societies and friends or relatives abroad, shipping these paupers to this country, have, whenever practicable, been notified of their return, and no complaint has been made that any of them have been improperly removed. It should be added, that of the paupers thus returned to their European homes, no cases have reappeared, and this state, and its cities and counties, have thereby been relieved of their permanent maintenance and care."

Illiteracy in the United States is vastly increased by immigration. It could hardly be otherwise. The immigrants are from the lower classes, where illiteracy is always most prevalent; many of them are from countries like Italy, Hungary, and French Canada, where the population at best is ignorant. The result is that in many of our Northern States where schools have been established and cherished for many years there is a steady increase of illiteracy from decade to decade. The census of 1880 reported that 9.4 per cent of the white population above the age of ten years could neither read nor write. But while of the native white population of that age only 8.7 per cent were illiterate, of the foreign born white population of that age 12 per cent could neither read nor write. In the Southern States the illiteracy was greater among the native white than among the foreign born. That is due to the general lack of education in that section and the degraded condition of the poor whites before the war. In the Northern States, wherever there has been a considerable immigration, the illiteracy is higher among the foreign than among the native born. That is the case in the states of

Massachusetts, Rhode Island, Connecticut, New York, Pennsylvania and many others.

Take the state of Massachusetts, for instance, where the foreign elements are well defined. The total number of illiterates in that state in 1885 was 122,263, but of these only 13,898 were native born, while 108,365 (88.63 per cent) were foreign born.[1] By illiterates is meant those (above the age of ten) who cannot read, or cannot write, or can neither read nor write, *any* language. But besides these there were many who could not read and write English although they could read and write some other language. There were not less than 30,883 such persons, almost all foreign born.[2] There were 18,231 persons (including French Canadians) who could read and write French, 6525 who could read and write German, 898 who could read and write Italian, 850 who could read and write Portuguese, and 3146 who could read and write Swedish, although none of these persons could read and write English. In Massachusetts therefore there were over 138,000 persons among the foreign born of the age of ten years and over, who could not read and write English.

Illiteracy in Massachusetts is due almost entirely to the presence of the foreign born. Of the native born ten years of age and over only a small fraction, (1.29

---

[1] Census of Massachusetts, 1885, vol. 1, part 2, p. lxxi.
[2] Census of Massachusetts, vol. 1, part 2, p. xcix.

per cent,) were illiterate, while of the foreign born of that age not less than 21.50 per cent were totally illiterate, while 27.50 per cent could neither read nor write English. Since 1875 the illiteracy among the native born has decreased, while among the foreign born it has increased. When therefore it is stated that 7.73 per cent of the people of Massachusetts are illiterate, this is due to no fault of the school system but to immigration.

The illiteracy among the foreign born is practically incurable because they are for the most part advanced in life. Of the 108,365 foreign born illiterates, more than 100,000 are twenty years of age and over, that is, beyond the age when they can go to school. This is the incurable illiteracy which will never be removed. Of the native born illiterates only 9530 are twenty years of age and over, a very small fraction of the total population.

The illiteracy among the foreign born of Massachusetts is due most largely to two nationalities, the Irish and the French Canadians. Of the 108,356 illiterates among the foreign born ten years of age and over, not less than 67,169 were born in Ireland, and 24,190 were French Canadians.[1] Of all the illiterates in Massachusetts those of Irish birth make up 54.95 per cent and those of French Canadian birth 19.78 per cent. Of the Irish in Massachusetts ten

[1] Census of Massachusetts, p. lxxxviii.

years of age and over, 27.85 per cent are illiterate, showing a greater illiteracy than is common among the foreign born. Of the French Canadians of the age of ten years and over, 41.39 per cent are totally illiterate, while 29.06 per cent can read or write French but not English, leaving only 29.55 per cent who can read or write English; that is, less than one-third. The case of the Italians is similar although less serious because the absolute number is as yet small. But of the Italians already in Massachusetts, 49.88 per cent are totally illiterate, 24 per cent can read or write Italian but not English, leaving only 26.12 per cent who can read and write English.[1]

These figures show what a very serious evil the people of Massachusetts have to contend with owing to the influx of this ignorant foreign element. The evil tends to correct itself in the second generation because the children of persons of foreign birth may take advantage of free schools and learn to read and write. But it is a difficult task to educate these children coming from ignorant households, and they are very apt to lose the little education they get, when they return to work among their people. Still further, the statistics seem to show that the tendency to illiteracy extends to the second generation. For of the 13,898 native born illiterates, not less than 7924 were of foreign, mixed or unknown parentage.

[1] Census of Massachusetts, vol. 1, part 2, p. 1142.

Of all the illiterates in Massachusetts only 5974 were of native parentage. It does seem as if the people of Massachusetts, had they had only their own ignorance to struggle with, would have reduced illiteracy to a mere shadow, — an unavoidable accompaniment of those various phases of misfortune such as pauperism, insanity, idiocy and defective physical condition which will never be entirely extirpated.

So far statistics carry us and no farther. They take notice only of overt acts or of the presence of certain capacities or incapacities. They cannot measure disposition or social inclination. We read in them, however, indications that the social health of the community is suffering, in some measure at least, by this influx of foreigners, — that the struggle of the community with unsocial and deteriorating elements is made, in some measure at least, more difficult. It is said that you cannot draw an indictment against a whole nation. In the same way you cannot say that any section of the whole community is an unmitigated evil. Even the negro has his place in our social economy, and one it would perhaps be difficult to fill. But you have a perfect right to say that the presence of certain elements or the characteristics of certain portions of the population make social development more difficult. It is in this sense that we study the social effects of immigration.

And, leaving the field of statistics, we cannot close our eyes to the fact that those national traits enumerated in the first chapter, such as respect for law and order, self-reliance, humane treatment of women and children, good temper, etc., which are none the less real for being incapable of exact measurement, are not likely to be strengthened in the first instance by the introduction of some of these foreign elements. These traits are the fruit of democracy, and the lower elements of the population of Europe have not been trained to them. The Irish Molly Maguires of the Pennsylvania coal fields have been succeeded by the Poles and Hungarians who now represent the elements of violence and disorder. In every socialistic labor party there is an extreme wing, — anarchistic or revolutionary, — which is always led by persons of foreign birth. The demand for state interference and regulation, which seems unnecessary to the Anglo-Saxon, seems perfectly natural to the German who has for centuries been living under paternal government. The French Canadian sees no reason why wife and child should be kept out of the factory, and has ideas of home life repugnant to the New Englander. The habit of seeking vengeance for personal wrongs with the stiletto clings to the immigrant from South Italy after he reaches this country, although it is repugnant to the character of our people in their more temperate climate. The habits of life and methods of living of many of the immigrants are undoubtedly below what economic prosperity has enabled us to establish in this country. It is foolish to maintain that these are desirable elements to be added to our social life.

CHAPTER IX.

ASSISTED EMIGRATION AND IMMIGRATION.

EMIGRATION has been viewed with different feelings at different periods. During the middle ages it was considered a loss to the community to have its members change their domicile. It was feared that the population of the country might be diminished; or trade secrets be carried into other lands; or the military strength of the home country be weakened. Over-population was not felt, and countries looked upon each other as rivals and possible enemies. Public opinion was in consequence hostile to emigration and active measures were taken to prevent it. It was only in exceptional cases, such as religious persecution, that it occurred, and the state stood by indifferent or opposed to it. Thus the cities of Switzerland forbade emigration:—Basel as early as 1767, Zurich in 1770, Schaffhausen in 1817. The Swiss government early directed its consuls to watch the fate of Swiss emigrants, and it published the reports of these consuls detailing the hardships which the emigrants endured in the strange country.[1]

[1] Karrer, Das Schweizerische Answanderungswesen. S. 7.

Two considerations induced men to look with more favor on emigration. One was colonial interests; the other was the tempting opportunity to get rid of worthless members of the community. The great colonial powers desired to see their colonies grow in population for the sake of the increased trade and commerce thereby brought to the home country. This induced economists, especially the English, to take the position that emigration was a good thing both for the home country and for the emigrant. The former gained a market for its goods; the latter bettered his own economic condition and produced cheaper food for those that remained behind.[1] The rapid introduction of machinery made good the loss of labor. Still, most governments did not feel called upon either to hinder or to encourage the movement.

In course of time another and more subtle motive has revealed itself. In small and poor communities the burden of supporting those unable to work has always been severely felt. By emigration there seemed to be a way of escaping it. The poor, with a little financial aid, might be sent on a journey from which they would never return to trouble the commune. In some cases there may have

---

[1] Fawcett, Political Economy, p. 145. Emigration, however, would cease to be a remedy for over-population as soon as the colonies became thickly settled. p. 235.

been a hope that these persons would really find an opportunity to begin a more prosperous career. The poor themselves were often anxious to go, being deluded by false and exaggerated reports of the chances for success in the countries beyond the sea. It was easy to accede to these desires and by a small advance of money at the present moment to escape the future support of the paupers. The Swiss cantons seem to have been the first to hit on this expedient. As early as 1854 the Swiss federal government notified the cantons that the United States was complaining of the sending of paupers and helpless people from Switzerland, and that the communes must be more careful or repressive measures might follow. As time went on the federal government tried to restrain the emigration of poor Swiss because they became a burden to the Swiss consuls in America to whom they were constantly applying for relief. The assistance was still continued by the cantons and by charitable societies, so that in 1855 it was said that of a total number of 2000 Swiss emigrants one-half had been assisted. The federal administration had no power to interfere until the law of 1880 was passed giving it the right to regulate agencies.

With this disposition on the part of local governing bodies it is not surprising that cases are constantly coming to light where unfit persons have been assisted to leave their homes. To the petty burgomaster mind, intent on saving a few francs in taxation, the temptation to "assist" a pauper to remove himself from the locality and thus free the poor funds from the burden of his support must oftentimes be well-nigh irresistible. And this can be accomplished in such indirect ways, and it is so difficult to distinguish between the pauper and the man who is merely poor, that it is almost impossible to detect such cases. Then again in the case of criminals, it is so easy for the police authorities simply to intimate to doubtful characters that it is better for them to betake themselves to places where they are not known, and even to furnish them a ticket with that end in view, that it is a wonder they do not resort to such expedients more frequently. It is not probable that one-tenth of these cases ever come to light; or they are discovered only when we inquire into the past history of criminals detected in this country. A few typical instances may be mentioned here.

The most celebrated case occurred while Mr. Nicholas Fish was United States Chargé d'Affaires at Berne. Mr. Fish learned incidentally that one of the cantons had paid the passage to America of an imbecile pauper. He immediately telegraphed to the United States consul at Liverpool who notified the steamship company and the man was returned.

The incident gave rise to considerable correspondence between the two governments and resulted in stricter surveillance of intending emigrants.[1]

According to the testimony of a Mr. Wolff before the Ford Immigration committee (p. 106) there exists in Munich a society for the purpose of assisting discharged convicts to begin life again. The object is surely an excellent one, but one means of effecting it is to send the persons out of the country. According to its own reports the society assisted, in the year 1883 alone, twenty-seven discharged convicts who wished to emigrate, and its branches in the provinces five others; and in 1884 the society assisted twenty-five such emigrants and the branches five others. In Boston the agent of the State Board of Lunacy and Charity testified (p. 558) that he had detected two cases of discharged convicts who had been assisted by British authorities to come to this country. These cases are isolated ones. It is extremely difficult to detect them, as often the only testimony is from the criminal himself who will of course deny that he has ever before been the inmate of a prison.

During recent years emigration of paupers and poor people from Europe has been assisted in various

---

[1] Many similar cases will be found mentioned in the correspondence between the State Department and Mr. Fish. Foreign Relations of United States, 1879–1881.

Assisted Emigration and Immigration. 173

ways: — By poor-law authorities; by charitable societies and persons; by remittances and prepaid tickets from relatives and friends in this country; and by steamship agents and brokers who have made it a business to induce people to emigrate and have advanced money to them or paid their passages and collected the sum after their arrival. When we take all these together we shall see that a very large percentage of the immigration is stimulated in various ways.

The British government has been the most active in assisting paupers and poor persons to emigrate. It has done so for the purpose of colonization and to relieve the pressure of population, especially in the poorer districts of Ireland and Scotland. According to a memorandum of the Local Government Board, of September, 1886, the poor-law guardians have always had the right since the Poor Law act of 1834 to use money from the rates for the purpose of assisting paupers to emigrate. They can even assist poor persons who have not yet come on the rates, except that "no orphan or deserted children can be deported unless they have actually come on the rates."[1] From 1851 to 1886 the number of persons thus assisted was 40,154, and the total amount of money spent was £152,902.[2]

---

[1] Reports of U. S. Consuls, pp. 375 and 458. See Aschrott, English Poor Law System, pp. 42 and 200.

In Ireland, as early as 1849, poor-law guardians were authorized to borrow money for the purpose of assisting emigration. By the Land act of 1881, the Land Commission was authorized to advance to poor-law guardians, by way of a loan, money to assist emigration, especially of families from the poorer and more thickly populated districts of Ireland. The amount was not to exceed £200,000 and not more than one-third was to be spent in any one year. By the Arrears of Rent act (1882), the Commissioner of Public Works was allowed to make grants in aid of emigration in certain districts where the union could not make adequate provision. The money was to come from the Irish Church temporalities fund and was not to exceed £100,000, or £5 to each person assisted. The following year (Tramways act) the amounts were raised to £200,000 and £8, respectively. In 1887 the Local Government Board at Dublin reported that there was still an unexpended balance of £23,000 which could be devoted to this purpose and that emigrants had been selected to go.

The United States government had already protested against assisted emigration of paupers, and the Local Government Board had sent out instructions that in future only those should be selected and aided who could show by letters that they had friends on this side of the water who would be willing to receive and assist them when once landed. It was felt to be doubtful if the United States government would willingly receive even such assisted immigrants, and the British minister in Washington was directed to make inquiry as to this of the State Department. Mr. Bayard in answer quoted the law of 1882, which says that "if on examination there should be found . . . any person unable to take care of himself or herself without becoming a public charge, they [the officers] shall report the same in writing to the collector of the port, and such persons shall not be permitted to land." Then after saying that each case would have to be determined on its merits, the Secretary goes on to say:

"In view of this policy and these laws, this Government could not fail to look with disfavor and concern upon the sending to this country, by foreign governmental agencies and at the public cost, of persons not only unlikely to develop qualities of thrift and self-support, but sent here because it is assumed that they have 'friends' in this country able to 'help and support' them. The mere fact of poverty has never been regarded as an objection to an immigrant, and a large part of those who have come to our shores have been persons who relied for support solely upon the exercise of thrift and manual industry; and to such persons, it may be said, the development of this country has in a large degree been due. But persons whose only escape from becoming and remaining a charge upon the community is the expected, but entirely contingent, voluntary help and support of friends, are not a desirable accession to our population, and their exportation hither by a foreign government, in order to get rid of the burden of their support, could scarcely be regarded as a friendly act, or in harmony with existing Laws."[1]

Notwithstanding this attitude of the United States government, the assisted emigrants were sent forward. In Philadelphia those who had letters from friends were allowed to land. In New York they were detained by the commissioners of emigration, but the steamship company sued out a writ of *habeas corpus* and they were released by Judge Brown on the ground that the commissioners in detaining them simply because they had been "assisted" had gone out of the statute. It appears therefore that under the present law the mere fact of having been "assisted" is not sufficient to prevent immigrants landing, but the commissioners must have reason to believe that the persons are "unable to support themselves without becoming a public charge."[2]

In connection with this governmental "assisted" emigration two societies have come into prominence in England with the same object in view. One is the so-called Tuke Committee which was originated by and is under the direction of Mr. James H. Tuke; and the other is the National Association for promoting State-Directed Emigration and Colonization,

---

[1] Correspondence relating to the Admission into the United States of Destitute Aliens and State-Assisted Emigrants. London, 1887.

[2] See Correspondence, etc. Also testimony of Commissioner Charles N. Taintor, Ford Immigration Committee, p. 266.

of which Lord Brabazon is president. The Tuke Committee[1] was organized in 1882 for the purpose of assisting families to emigrate in order to relieve the distress existing in certain congested districts of Ireland. In the spring of that year the Committee sent to various destinations in Canada and the United States nearly 1500 persons, about 260 families, not in any way assisted either by the government or by Poor-Law Unions. In 1883, when the government, strongly urged thereto by the Committee, took up the emigration question, Lord Spencer requested the Committee to undertake the emigration from certain distressed districts in the counties of Mayo and Galway, which they consented to do, as well as to supplement the capitation grant made by the government. During the two following years the Committee with the aid of the government sent out over 1000 families or nearly 8000 persons. During the same period about 16,000 persons were assisted by government agencies. Owing to the cooperation of the Tuke Committee with the government the two classes of emigrants became confused, and the hostility which was excited on account of the government-assisted emigrants extended itself to those sent out by the Committee, and it was obliged to suspend operations.

[1] State Aid to Emigrants by J. H. Tuke, The Nineteenth Century, Feb. 1885.

As to the character of these "assisted" emigrants there is conflicting testimony. Mr. Tuke asserts that his committee sent out no paupers and that they carefully examined every emigrant they assisted. "They were seen on at least three or more occasions by members of the Committee and every possible information about them was obtained from the doctor, the relieving officer, or other responsible persons best acquainted with each particular district." The emigrants had their railroad fares to the interior paid after they landed and were provided with a sum of money in addition. Mr. Tuke quotes letters from Bishop Ireland of Minnesota, Sir Charles Tupper, High Commissioner for Canada, and others, speaking of the good character of the immigrants and the general success that attended the effort.

On the other hand, there were distinct complaints made by the Canadian authorities that the immigrants were not what they had been represented to be, and the colonial government withdrew the encouragement which it had at first given the undertaking. Proof of this is seen in the letter addressed by the Secretary of the Department of Immigration, Ontario, to Mr. H. Hodgkin, of Mr. Tuke's Emigration Committee, from which the following extracts are made.[1]

---

[1] Lord Brabazon, State-Directed Emigration, The Nineteenth Century, Nov. 1884. See also testimony of Dr. Charles S. Hoyt, Ford Immigration Committee, p. 238.

"It was deemed advisable to wait and see how the immigrants sent out last year under the auspices of the Imperial government would fare during the winter, before encouraging more of the same class to follow. So far their condition is not encouraging, as many of them are living on charity, and public feeling has been somewhat strongly expressed, in the public press and otherwise, concerning them. This remark really applies to the people sent out by the unions, but they are so closely associated in the public mind with those sent out by you, that it will be hard to find employment for either class next summer, as the farmers place but little value on their labor, and the people of the cities are afraid of laying the foundations of pauperism. What makes matters worse, a considerable number of families who went to the United States last summer have been sent back to Toronto, and have now to be supported by charity.

"The Ontario government has therefore decided that it will no longer be possible to give assistance to any class of workhouse or union people either in the way of meals or railway passes.

"The numbers of union or workhouse people sent out appear to the Commissioner to have considerably exceeded the number of that class suggested by Major Gaskell, when here, as likely to be forwarded. They are also inferior as a class to those described by him. . . . The difficulties arising in selection are quite understood and appreciated. For these reasons it will not be possible any longer to continue the arrangement made with Major Gaskell in reference to the workhouse or union people who may be forwarded, and therefore the special privileges which they have been granted under that arrangement must necessarily be withdrawn.

"I take the opportunity of stating, for the benefit of your committee, that while there is ample room in this province for all able-bodied persons of both sexes who are willing and able to work, yet these two features are essential to the procuring of a livelihood here, namely, ability and willingness to labor. Many persons in the older countries drift into the workhouse from their inability or their unwillingness to earn a livelihood by labor. It is impossible to provide a home here for such people."

The other society, of which Lord Brabazon is president, has a much more ambitious scheme. It desires that the government shall advance money to persons willing to emigrate, this money to be repaid by the emigrants and then used again for the same purpose. Lord Brabazon calculates that a sum of one hundred pounds sterling would be sufficient to remove a family to Canada and settle it on a farm granted by the Dominion government. If the government would start with a grant of 1,000,000 pounds, 10,000 families could thus be removed in one year, and the congestion of population in the east end of London and the large cities be relieved. The association has the backing of many influential men and the support of trade-unions representing 150,000 members. It has appealed to both a Liberal and a Conservative ministry but has found little support from either, the ministers doubting the practicability of the scheme and whether the colonial governments would acquiesce in it. In February, 1887, a Parliamentary committee consisting of 32 members of the House of Lords and 135 members of the House of Commons was formed to favor state-assisted emigration. They formulated a colonization scheme which was submitted through the colonial office to the various governments. It met with a very chilling reception, most of the colonial governments declining to have anything to do with it.[1]

The difficulty with all these schemes of assisted emigration is the suspicion which the colonial governments cannot help entertaining that they are attempts to get rid of undesirable members of the home community and foist them on to the new countries. Lord Brabazon protests very vigorously against this in the article quoted above:

"And here it would be well to make it clearly understood that the advocates of the state direction of emigration, as represented at all events by the National Association for promoting State-directed Emigration and Colonization, of which I have the honor to be chairman, do not propose that her Majesty's government should transfer the idle, the vicious, the ne'er do well, or the pauper from the slums of London to those of Melbourne or Toronto (as seems to be the idea of some of the opponents of state emigration), nor has it ever been proposed that any individual should be sent to the colonies either contrary to his or her desire, or without the concurrence of the authorities of these colonies, nor is there any intention of making a money present to any emigrant to enable him to proceed to the colonies.

"All that the association desires is that the British government shall, in conjunction with the colonial authorities, draw up

[1] Correspondence from Colonial Governments in answer to Memorandum by Parliamentary Colonization Committee of May 1, 1888, London, 1889.

a well-considered scheme of emigration and colonization, by means of which *able-bodied and industrious men who may not possess the means necessary for them to emigrate*, shall be provided with the means of emigrating with their families, or of colonizing, *under the strictest possible guarantee that the money shall be repaid with easy interest* within a certain number of years."

If this programme were strictly carried out, the resulting emigration would not be an injury to the colony receiving it, especially as Lord Brabazon proposes to regulate it by an Imperial commission, on which each colony shall be represented but from which it may withdraw at any time, whereupon the flow of emigrants to that particular colony shall immediately cease. It is safe to say that public opinion in the colonies, which is overwhelmingly under the control of the laboring class, would demand such withdrawal whenever the slightest inconvenience was felt or supposed to be felt from the influx of labor. In fact it is easy to imagine that, were such a commission once established, the colonies might demand that its functions should be extended to unassisted emigration, so that they might control the whole matter. In such a case the position of England with its surplus labor would be worse than ever.

But it is not easy to see exactly how the commission or the society is going to select only the able-bodied and industrious workmen. In voluntary emigration, the fact that the man has obtained money enough to emigrate is some evidence that he is able-bodied and thrifty; although the value of this evidence is being steadily diminished by the low cost of the passage and the remittances of friends, — as Lord Derby pointed out in his speech in the House of Lords, March 29, 1884:

> "Probably there was not a village in the country from which one or two persons had not emigrated, and these persons communicated with their friends at home; thus ignorance as to the advantages of emigration diminishes, while with more rapid and more complete communication the risks of an emigrant's life would tend to decrease."

But when the state advances the money, this test of the emigrant's fitness to emigrate is taken away, even if the money is nominally a loan; and one does not see exactly what is to take its place. The agent of the government or of the colony will be able to distinguish, perhaps, the really criminal, the actually infirm or crippled, and those who have been paupers; but he will not be able to discern whether a man is an indolent vagabond, or morally vicious and good for nothing. And if the government is to send only those who are industrious and thrifty, will it really afford relief to over-population? And will not its action be open to the objection urged by Professor Rogers, that the cream of the population will be expatriated? The difficulty is evidently felt by the members of the society, and they find it hard to satisfy both the home people who want to get rid of the poor and worthless, and the colonists who want only the good and industrious. The difficulty comes out very naïvely in the speech of the Earl of Carnarvon, in advocating the scheme before the House of Lords, in which he said:

> "It was sometimes said that in sending out emigrants by the aid of the state you would choose the best man. He should be sorry to see the best men leave the country, but there was an intermediate class who were easily convertible into excellent workmen and good colonists."

But will the colonies be content with this newly defined "middle working class," when by voluntary emigration they may get the "upper working class," or even members of the "lower middle class"?

In fact the interests of the colony and of the mother country in this matter are antithetical. State and charity assisted emigration will need to be carefully watched from this side of the water. They can accomplish their real object only by sending out persons whose worth to the country receiving them may well be questioned. The tendency will always be to consider the poverty of the applicant rather than his capacity to become a good citizen in the colonies. And it is not quite safe to trust the choice of our citizens to a body of foreign officials whose interests are not at all identical with ours and never can be.[1]

There is another form of encouraging emigration from the other side of the water, which, in many of its aspects, scarcely deserves to be ranked under the head of "assisted," while in other phases it reveals the most demoralizing influence, deserving the sever-

[1] Various other societies and individuals assist emigrants to leave the country. Thus the London Times (Jan. 31, 1889) says: "That the Prisoners' Aid Society assists convicts to emigrate everybody knows, and probably the United States receives its full quota of the persons so aided." No fewer than 38 persons and societies are mentioned in the U. S. Consular Reports (p. 602) as assisting pauper children to settle in Canada. In 1881, there were brought to Canada 727 immigrants, chiefly children, by such societies and individuals; in 1882, 1048; in 1883, 1218; in 1884, 2011; in 1885, 1746. The experiment has not always been successful. See Aschrott, English Poor Law, p. 225, and Ford Immigration Committee, testimony of Mr. Wrightington, p. 546. The Central Emigration Society at its sixth annual meeting (1889) announced that the restrictions placed on the emigration of pauper children by the Local Government Board had been removed, and that the managers of reformatory and industrial schools were to be allowed to apply treasury grants under certain conditions to the fitting out and emigrating of such children. London Times, July 19, 1889.

In Sweden, philanthropic societies have paid the passage of liberated criminals to America, but such practices have now generally ceased. U. S. Consular Reports, p. 331. Lady Cathcart sent out one year 12 crofter families, and the following year 45 families to Canada. In 1864, 557 Paisley weavers were assisted to emigrate by various public and private societies. Tuke, State-Aided Emigration. The Jewish Board of Guardians (a private charitable organization in London) assisted during the five years, 1882–1886, 8429 poor Jews, mostly Russian, to go on to America. Report from House of Commons Committee on Immigration.

est condemnation and the strictest measures of repression. I refer to the assistance sent back from this country by emigrants and persons already here. This assistance takes on one of two forms, either of remittances of money to friends and relatives at home in order to enable them to come, or of prepaid tickets. Of the amount of money sent back to Great Britain I have already spoken in another place. There is a steady stream of money going from this country to be used largely for the purpose of bringing persons here.

The best way, however, to bring one's friend to this country is to purchase a prepaid ticket and send it to him, together with a small sum of money to pay his incidental expenses. In the stress of competition the steamship companies have been very eager to sell these tickets and for that purpose have agents all through this country. Thus the Inman Steamship Company has not less than 3400 such agents, and thirty-three per cent of all its steerage passengers come on prepaid tickets. On the Hamburg-American line forty per cent of the passages are prepaid. The Anchor line has 2500 agents in this country, and fifty per cent of the passages are prepaid. On the Guion line, twenty-five per cent; on the National line, twenty-five per cent; on the North German Lloyd, from thirty to forty per cent; on the Fabre line, thirty-three per cent; on the Cunard line, fifteen per cent; and on the Red Star line, ten per cent of the passages are prepaid. These figures show that the management of emigration is very largely in the hands of persons on this side of the water. The price of the passage is regulated by the competition of the steamship companies here, and is high or low according as they come to an agreement as to rates or fight each other for the purpose of getting the traffic. It is not fixed according to the competition of the emigrants on the other side nor according to the cost of the service. The prevailing rate is from twenty-three to twenty-six dollars, of which three dollars commonly goes to the agent as his commission.[1]

That it is perfectly desirable and natural for an immigrant who has prospered in this country to send for his wife and family is not to be denied. The family feeling is one that should in every way be encouraged, and we can only rejoice in the prosperity of these new citizens who labor and save in order to accomplish this end. That when they prosper they should desire to send for the aged parents or the weak and helpless members of the family, who were not able to brave the uncertainties and dangers of the first voyage, is also altogether commendable. The same loving care that sent for them will support them when they get here. There are instances

[1] Testimony of steamship agents before the Ford Immigration Committee, pp. 1–56.

where persons have paid the passages of helpless relatives to this country simply to throw them on our poor-rates because they fare better here than at home, but such cases are doubtless rare. That a man should send for his able-bodied brothers and sisters or his old acquaintances is no danger to the community. He commonly has a place for them either in his own occupation or in some other. This thing regulates itself. In bad times he will not encourage his friends to come. All such assistance to immigration is natural and can scarcely be stopped without violating the highest instincts of the human heart. Mistakes are sometimes made and more persons brought than are needed, but with our expanding prosperity a place is finally found for them all.

These facilities for purchasing prepaid tickets have developed, however, a business which results in assistance being given to immigration from purely commercial motives. The rivalry of steamship companies led to the employment of numerous agents, or rather to the payment of commissions to any person who would sell tickets. Books of tickets were placed in the hands of so-called bankers (exchangers), boarding-house keepers and even liquor sellers, in short, of those persons who came into contact with immigrants or to whom they would naturally look for aid and advice. For every ticket sold the agent received a commission. It was perfectly natural that these agents should use their influence to persuade immigrants to send for their relatives and friends, promising to secure work for them when they arrived. In many cases they sacrificed a part of the commission in order to sell the ticket. In other cases they even advanced the money under the promise of repayment out of the first earnings of the new arrivals. A further step naturally suggested itself,—namely, to have a correspondent, or agent, or partner on the other side of the water to sell the tickets to intending emigrants. The Italian agents introduced a still further modification in order to make the business more profitable. Although there was much competition among the regular steamship companies, still, either in self-defence or sometimes by agreement, they did maintain the rate of fare at a certain point. The brokers would, however, occasionally find a "tramp" steamer that would take emigrants at less than the regular rate in order to make a cargo. They chose therefore to issue their own tickets which entitled the purchaser to a passage to America, but at a time designated by the agent. If they could find a "tramp" steamer, the emigrant would be brought down to the port of departure and put on board. If no "tramp" steamer appeared, these tickets could be exchanged for tickets by some one of the regular lines.

By these means a regular brokerage business was established, the evil effects of which can easily be imagined and which have been exemplified in the case of immigration from Italy. On the other side of the water we have a body of men whose object is to persuade men to emigrate by holding out the expectation that profitable employment will be found for them by the "man" in America who is the agent's principal. The peasant is persuaded to sell or mortgage his little farm or vineyard, in many cases to leave his family, under the firm belief that work is so plentiful and so well-paid in America that he will have no difficulty in sending for them or in supporting them until he can return with a competence. In some cases, where the emigrant has no property, his passage is paid by the agent, and he promises to repay a larger sum out of his earnings, the excess over the cost of the passage serving as compensation for commission, interest and risk. On this side of the water we have a body of men who receive the immigrants on their arrival and upon whom they are absolutely dependent owing to their contract (which they observe religiously), and on account of their ignorance of the language and the country. These men exploit the immigrants in a variety of ways. They board and lodge them in the most wretched manner, making enormous rents; they loan them money at usurious rates; they sell them bills of ex-

Assisted Emigration and Immigration. 191

change and prepaid passages for their families; they find them employment, receiving a bonus which is euphemistically termed a "present"; they furnish bodies of laborers to railroad companies, receiving at the same time the contract for boarding and lodging them, the company deducting the board-money from the wages of the laborers. So numerous are these sources of profit that it seems as if the agents were not particularly concerned as to the quick repayment of the original passage money; for it appears that although there were three or four thousand Italians in New York unable to obtain work still others were constantly brought over.

The investigation of the Ford committee showed that the business as above described of assisting immigrants to come to this country was literally the case with Italian immigration. The steamship agents, although with apparent reluctance, testified that they had been accustomed to sell tickets in books or bunches. Lately they had made a practice of selling only a limited number to any one person and only with the names filled out. Their object in doing this was apparently to prevent business accumulating in the hands of single persons who would employ "tramp" steamers. But the testimony of immigrants showed that it was the custom of agents in Italy to collect a number of persons, conduct them to Naples and there put them on board of a steamer, the intending emigrant having no previous knowledge of the ship or the time of sailing. The emigrants also testified that they were promised work at high wages on their arrival, and that these promises had not been fulfilled. Thus Angelo Antonio di Dierro testified (p. 100) that he had been persuaded to emigrate by a man of the name of Di Chiccio who had represented that work was plentiful in America at $1.50 a day, and that his passage had been paid on his entering into an engagement to repay 200 francs. The cost of a ticket at that time was 115 francs. Another Italian (p. 120) had sold his mule in order to purchase a ticket to America, but had found no work since he arrived. A third (p. 131) owned a little vineyard worth 400 or 500 francs and had entered into a written obligation to return 250 francs for his ticket before the first of August. He had been unable to find work since he landed and was under the apprehension that his vineyard would be seized in payment of the debt and his family turned out. A fourth owned a house worth 300 francs and had entered into a similar obligation to return 250 francs, but had been unable to find work since landing. Many others related similar experiences. Most of the Italian witnesses expressed a desire to return to Italy, saying they had been deceived in regard to finding work here and that they were much better off at home. Other witnesses brought out the fact that these men could get work only by paying the contractors, and that they were plundered by the contractors who received the privilege of boarding them, so that it was a long time before they could get out of debt.

It is needless to say that this whole business of inducing men to emigrate is an abuse, hurtful to the emigrants themselves and to this country which has a lot of ignorant, unskilled laborers landed on its shores unable to take care of themselves and entirely at the mercy of these brokers and contractors. It is for the interest of both Italy and America to stop this fraudulent and deceitful business.

One other kind of assisted emigration remains to be noticed only because it is of historic interest. Until within a few years countries in the new world have desired immigration and have even assisted it. The British colonies have been particularly active in this respect. In 1870 the various North American governments, including the Dominion itself, spent $97,281 for the purpose of assisting immigration. In 1874 the provincial governments agreed to unite their efforts in order to make them more effective, and entered into an agreement by which the minister of agriculture of the Dominion was vested for a series of years with the duty of promoting immigration. A high commissioner was appointed, with offices in London and agents located at the principal seaports, viz., Glasgow, Dublin, Belfast and Bristol.

Agents have also been stationed at different times at Paris, at Hamburg and in Switzerland. Travelling or lecturing agents have been employed, and at one time it is said there were not less than thirty-five of these missionaries in the field. In addition to these measures, passages were paid in whole or in part for certain kinds of immigrants; they were met on arrival by agents, their railroad fares paid to points in the interior, and free grants of land made to them.[1] Since 1878 efforts to induce immigration have slackened, and in April, 1888, the system of assisted passages ceased altogether.[2]

The Australian colonies have also paid the passages in whole or in part of desirable immigrants. In the colony of New South Wales the number of assisted immigrants in 1883 was 8369. That was the maximum number for any year. In 1885 the number was only 5554.[3]

Similar efforts to induce immigration have been made by Mexico, Brazil, Chili, Argentine, and various states in the United States.[4] These efforts have consisted for the most part in spreading information about the resources of the country and in making grants of land to intending settlers. But with the

[1] Reports of U. S. Consuls on Immigration, pp. 456, 568 and 575.
[2] Board of Trade Journal, June, 1889.
[3] Reports of U. S. Consuls, p. 710.
[4] Numerous state bureaux to encourage immigration were established in 1864, towards the close of the war.

new disposition to restrict immigration most of these efforts have been abandoned. There is, however, at the present time a movement in the southern states to attract immigrants, especially to the state of Texas.[1]

[1] SOUTHERN IMMIGRATION ASSOCIATION. — A representative gathering of southern men was held at Hot Springs, N. C., recently, at which delegates from eleven states appeared. The governors of the states of Virginia, South Carolina and Georgia were among those present. The purpose of the convention was to discuss the best practicable means to be employed in inducing a desirable class of immigrants to settle in the south. The result of the proceedings was the proposal to organize the Southern Immigration Association, with headquarters in New York city. Subscriptions of money in sums of $1000 each are to be invited. When the amount subscribed equals $20,000 a permanent organization will be formed by the subscribers. Southern railroads, manufacturing corporations, boards of trade and other trade and industrial bodies south of the Ohio and east of the Mississippi are expected to become contributors. Some idea as to the class of immigrants desired may be obtained from the following extract from an article in the Baltimore Manufacturers' Record: "One thing must be plainly understood at the outset. The south needs many more men of capital than it now has, whether that capital is in money, in intelligence or in skill in the mechanic arts. But it does not need mere muscle. There is enough unskilled labor for present requirements, and in all probability there will be for generations. The south has happily escaped the evils attendant upon the employment of foreign laborers at the north. It will lend no aid to any who may wish to bring that element into its borders. None but those who have the ability to maintain themselves and to participate in the grand procession of progress and industrial development will be welcome. The south makes no war upon foreigners as such, but it will object, and that most strenuously, to any attempt to foist upon it those who would, from their first coming into it, be an irreparable injury to the communities among whom they might settle." After describing the fine character of recent immigration from the northwest of English-

In response to the demands of the Association for State-directed Emigration, the British government has established an Emigrants' Information Office. The object of this office is not to render assistance in the way of paying passages, but simply to give information to any person who is thinking of emigrating to the colonies. It publishes and distributes circulars of information, answers letters of inquiry, reports on the condition of the labor market in the different colonies, the special demand existing for particular kinds of labor, etc. Its activity is useful, but there seems to be no very great increase in the demand for that sort of information. The office itself is very moderate in urging men to emigrate, and depicts the difficulties rather than the advantages of life in the colonies.

We have thus enumerated the various forms of assisted emigration in order to gain a notion of the numerous and powerful artificial forces stimulating

speaking immigrants, the Record says: " We want more such settlers. The south is the place for them, but not for the hordes who are coming by thousands weekly from European ports. We repeat, if those having the affairs of the Southern Immigration Society in charge will announce that their efforts will be directed solely to promoting the immigration of English-speaking people, they will receive all the moral and material support they desire. If, on the other hand, they establish agencies on the European continent, and attempt to pour into the south the same classes of immigrants that have been landing in New York and Canada for the last fifteen years, they will be opposed by nine-tenths of the southern people." Bradstreet's, May 12, 1888.

the movement of persons from the old world to the new. This enumeration dispels at once the illusion that the movement at the present time is a natural one in the sense that the individual initiates it of his own notion and carries it out by his own unaided powers. Emigration is sometimes spoken of as if it were simply the operation of the individual, coolly and rationally measuring the advantages to be gained, and thus advancing his own economic condition and that of the country to which he comes. Nothing could be further from the truth. Emigration proceeds now under numerous influences, the efforts of steamship companies, the urging of friends and relatives, the assistance of poor-law authorities and charitable societies, and the subtle but powerful influence of popular delusion in regard to the *el dorado* character of the new world, which has been created by these different interested parties.

The atmosphere of the old world is permeated with the spirit of emigration. In all cases of hardship, of lack of employment, of misery and want, of misfortune and crime, the sufferer is urged to emigrate. If an industry is languishing, the workmen are told to emigrate. If the poor-houses are crowded, the authorities try to empty them on the colonies. If the country is deserted for the city, the city is to be depleted for the colonies; and the persons who have once deserted the soil are to be placed on it again.

If population is constantly increasing by an excess of births over deaths, the remedy lies in cutting down at the other end by sending away the adults. There is something almost revolting in the anxiety of certain countries to get rid of their surplus population and to escape the burden of supporting the poor, the helpless and the depraved. And an equally painful although not equally blamable spectacle is now presented by the new countries refusing to admit these miserable beings, so that they are thrown like shuttlecocks from one side of the ocean to the other, no one willing to compassionate and afford them shelter.

It is plain that state and charity assisted emigration is destined to fail of its purpose. On a small scale it amounts to nothing one way or the other; it is no relief to the old country and no great danger to the new. But the moment it is prosecuted on a large scale the inevitable antithesis between the interests of the old and the new country appears, as was noted above. The old country wishes to get rid of the worse part of its population, — (it would be suicidal to send away the better), — while the new country absolutely refuses to receive that class. In 1849 the Australian colonies protested so vigorously against the further deportation to them of convicts from Great Britain that it was stopped. To-day the colonies and the United States have made the same protest against the deportation of paupers and helpless persons, and that will inevitably cease. It cannot be otherwise. The position of the new countries is perfectly impregnable on that point, and even if their position were lacking in logic, public opinion has been made up and it is useless to expect it to change.

But state-assisted emigration on such a scale as to relieve the pressure of over-population at home is impracticable, again, for economic reasons. There seems to be a popular impression, (doubtless a survival from earlier days), that all you have to do is to transport a man to the new world and that then his fortune is made. No fallacy could be more dangerous than this. It is only a select class of men who now succeed in the new world.[1] In many respects the competition is as keen and the labor market as

[1] "There is no colony where a man willing to work, able to work, and indifferent to the kind of work, will not get a living; but agriculturists should be warned that farm work at home is one thing, and in the colonies quite another, and that the conditions of country life in Canada, Australasia, and South Africa are, as a rule, far rougher and lonelier than in England.

"Men who have not been from their childhood engaged on the land must remember that in new countries there is not the same strong line drawn between different trades and different branches of the same trade as in our own; and that, therefore, the more specialized a man has become in his work and calling the less fitted he is to emigrate, partly because he is unlikely, in most cases, to find an opening in his own specialty in the colonies, partly because he is not well suited to turn his hand to general labor." Report of Emigrant's Information Office, 1888.

overcrowded as in Europe. In many cases capital is absolutely needed and mere manual labor is present in excess. The emigrant comes, ignorant of the methods of work, inexperienced in the climatic and other conditions, often helpless in resources, without friends, perhaps not even speaking the language. It is absolute cruelty to place him under these disadvantages in a struggle for existence. The notion that thousands of men can be thrust into such conditions without suffering themselves, and deranging the economy of the colony is perfectly absurd. Emigration at any rate needs no artificial stimulus. The movement is sufficiently great in itself.

CHAPTER X.

PROTECTING THE EMIGRANT: THE PASSENGERS' ACTS.

THE various nations of Europe have come finally, although some of them with reluctance, to permit freedom of migration. Under pressure from the United States they have abandoned the doctrine that a man can under no circumstances divest himself of his allegiance, and now by treaty they allow their citizens, after residence of five years and naturalization abroad, to re-appear as citizens of the new country. Citizenship has thus become a matter of choice, and any one can leave his own country and select a new one where he finds the conditions of living more favorable. There appears to be no reason why a man cannot become successively a citizen of different countries, as his desires or interests may dictate. And in fact there is such a lack of harmony in the laws of different countries, that in some cases it may be plausibly argued that a man is the citizen of two countries at the same time; and in other cases it seems as if he were the citizen of none.[1] It is not intended to enter upon the complicated and unfruit-

[1] This subject is discussed more fully in the final chapter.

ful discussion of the conflict of laws, but it is interesting to note the relation of the emigrant during the process of emigration, so to speak, to the country he is abandoning and the one he is adopting.

Freedom of emigration is not perfect even in the modern state. The intending emigrant often comes into conflict with the universal military duty. Where a young man has reached the age when he is liable to serve in the army, permission to emigrate will be refused him, and if he leave without permission a penalty will be entered against him to which he is liable when he returns, or his property is liable in case he leaves any behind. Even after he has served the term in the active service and entered the reserve, he is expected to present himself at the regular intervals for training, and must receive permission if he desire to absent himself. Where the state demands such a service of all its citizens it is impossible to allow some to evade it by simple absence, and it is unpatriotic in them to attempt it. Even when they absent themselves long enough to acquire citizenship in another country and then return, using that citizenship as an excuse to escape the burdens resting upon other members of the community, it is impossible for the state to look upon their position with favor. If they return with the intention of making their permanent residence at home, they are held to have forfeited their new citizenship and taken up the old. A residence of a certain time (generally two years) will be *prima facie* evidence that they intend to stay. So also it would seem that in the case of certain obligations imposed on the citizen by the civil law, such as the support of aged or infirm relatives, or the obligation to pay taxes, permission to emigrate would not be given until provision for the discharge of these had been made.

But the facilities for travel are so great at the present time that it is not difficult for the individual to escape these restrictions and leave without permission. In fact the greater number of emigrants do not take the trouble to procure a permit; and hundreds, if not thousands, leave for the express purpose of evading the military duty. There seems to be a probability, however, with the increasing tendency toward socialistic legislation, that this perfect freedom of the individual will be restricted. As the state does more and more for its citizens they will be bound up in associations from which it will be difficult for them to free themselves. We shall speak of this later when we come to discuss the abstract right to emigrate.

Even after the emigrant has started on his way, with the definite intention of abandoning his native country and seeking a new allegiance, he still remains an object of solicitude to the mother country. He is regarded as one of her citizens and entitled to her protection and care. This care is exercised first of all by the diplomatic and consular service which is instructed to look out for the interests of the emigrant in the foreign country, to help him in difficulties, and (in some cases) to send him home if he desires. As early as 1848 the Swiss government stationed a commissioner at Havre to watch over the interests of the numerous Swiss emigrants who shipped at that port. During many years we have the Swiss consuls sending information home as to the condition of Swiss immigrants in North and South America, and frequently appealing to be allowed to render assistance to unfortunates who wished to return to Switzerland. In the attempts to establish Swiss and German colonies in Brazil, the agents of the government have been active in seeing that the contracts were fair to the immigrants and the stipulations carried out. In some cases the home governments have made representations to the Brazilian government in behalf of the immigrants. The Italian consul in New York testified before the Ford committee that he had received a sum of money from the Italian government for the purpose of relieving the distress among the Italian immigrants who had been unable to obtain work. Belgium has recently established at Buenos Ayres an information bureau for the use of Belgian emigrants.[1]

[1] "The Belgian bureau at Buenos Ayres is required to give substantial assistance to emigrants from Belgium. It will give them information

The care of the state for the emigrant is exercised in a more general but at the same time more effective way by the so-called passengers' acts. When emigration first became extensive great abuses sprang up. The emigrants were crowded on board sailing ships, without sufficient room and with little regard to health, comfort and decency. As a consequence the maritime countries have found it necessary to enact laws containing minute regulations for the health and comfort of passengers, especially those in the steerage. These laws proceed it is true from general humanitarian and police considerations rather than from any care of a particular state for the welfare of its subjects, but they have had the effect of protecting the emigrant from the rapacity and greed of the individual ship-owner intent only on his profit.

As England was the first country to feel the great tide of emigration to the new world which began in the "forties," so it was one of the first to regulate the business of transporting emigrants. The passengers' act of 1852 was amended in 1855, and, with a

as to the practical means of finding as quickly as possible occupation under advantageous conditions; it will show them the centres where Belgian workers are already established; and it will constitute in fact a kind of labor exchange where those who come to offer their services will find all the information they desire.

"Further, the agent in charge of the bureau will remain as much as possible in relation with the emigrants established in the Argentine Republic, and will receive any complaints they may have to make for transmission to the Belgian Consulate." Board of Trade Journal, 1889.

few changes introduced in 1863, contains the most minute regulations of the way the emigrant passenger shall be treated. Some of the provisions are as follows: Every ship intending to carry emigrant passengers must be inspected as to sea-worthiness and compliance with the provisions of the law, and receive a certificate from the emigration officers before it sails; it shall carry passengers on only two decks; sailing vessels shall carry only one passenger to every two tons burthen; there shall be at least five superficial feet of upper deck room to each passenger for the purpose of exercise; the space between decks must be not less then six feet; there shall be not more than two tiers of berths between the decks, with a space of at least two feet and six inches between a berth and the bottom of the next one, or between a berth and the deck above; berths must be at least six feet long and two feet and six inches wide; male passengers above the age of fourteen, except when accompanied by their wives, must have a separate cabin securely separated from the other passengers; hospitals must be provided on the upper deck, at least eighteen superficial feet for every fifty passengers; every ship must carry a doctor and a supply of medicines and medical comforts; the quantity of water and provisions is minutely regulated according to the number of passengers and the probable length of the voyage;

there must be proper ventilation and sanitary arrangements; there must be stewards and cooks according to the number of passengers; offensive and dangerous cargoes shall not be carried, such as gunpowder, guano, vitriol, green hides, and cattle; the last are allowed under certain conditions. The act also provides for the maintenance of the passenger if sailing be delayed after the appointed time, or if he be delayed on the route or landed somewhere else than the port he engaged passage for; and provision is made for forwarding him if he be landed elsewhere than the port for which he engaged passage. Similar acts are now in force in all maritime countries, so that the emigrant is abundantly protected against overcrowding, sickness, hunger, and the brutality of officers or crews or fellow-passengers.

Of late years this protection of the emigrant has extended itself to the prevention of fraudulent misrepresentations for the purpose of inducing citizens to emigrate. It was found that emigration agents, whose only object was to sell tickets and get their commissions, deceived the ignorant peasants and artisans by glowing accounts of the conditions of living in the new countries, if not by actual misrepresentation of the assistance to be received by the immigrant from the communities across the sea. Many persons were thus induced to emigrate who were utterly unfit for colonial life, and who were immediately plunged into misery and want, and obliged to apply to the consuls for relief or become a burden on the charity of their countrymen abroad. The efforts of these agents introduced a restless spirit of discontent. In some cases they succeeded in creating a migratory movement which deranged the economic relations of whole districts, and even threatened to depopulate them. The home government could not look upon this process with indifference. It was assailed by the complaints of its consuls, of its citizens resident abroad who were obliged to relieve the distresses of their countrymen, and by the fears of employers of labor at home. As a consequence, the governments of Europe have recently been passing laws for the regulation of the business of emigration. The intent of these laws is that the business of soliciting emigrants and selling tickets shall be confined to responsible persons who shall enter into a prescribed contract with the emigrant, for the violation of which they can be held liable.

The English passengers' act of 1855 contained a provision that emigrant brokers should be licensed by the emigration commissioners and enter into a bond to the amount of one thousand pounds sterling; also that emigrant runners should be licensed by a justice of the peace and wear a badge. By the same act a form of contract was prescribed which was to be a part of the passage ticket of every emigrant. So also the various states of Germany have for a number of years had laws regulating the business of selling emigrant tickets. Generally these laws prescribe that the agent must be a German by birth; he must receive a license and deposit a sum of money as security; he must keep a register of the persons to whom he sells tickets; he must use a prescribed form of contract; he is not allowed to sell tickets for forwarding the emigrant beyond the landing place in the new country.[1] There is no uniform law for the German empire, although article four of the constitution gives to the imperial authorities the power of regulating emigration. There is a growing demand in Germany, however, that the empire shall take the matter in hand and pass a law regulating the whole business. The laws hitherto have probably been intended to prevent evasion of military service rather than to protect the emigrant or discourage emigration. Both of these latter motives would probably find expression in a new law.

Switzerland has been the first country to pass a comprehensive law to prevent the abuses of indiscriminate emigration, and to protect the citizen against the misrepresentations and solicitations of

[1] Altenberg, Deutsche Auswanderungsgesetzgebung, 1885.

the emigration agent. Her example has been followed by Italy, and will probably be followed by the other countries of Europe.[1] This legislation marks a new attitude on the part of the countries of Europe towards unrestricted emigration. It treats the act of changing one's domicile or the persuading another so to do as a very serious matter which is not to be undertaken except under guarantees to prevent mistakes and frauds. Still further, the measures intended to prevent the emigrant being deceived can easily be extended, (especially if there should happen to be a disposition on the part of the administration to extend them,) so as to be a restriction on emigration of a very effective kind. Taken in connection with the disposition of the United States and the British colonies to discourage immigration, these measures may lead to a modification of the right of free migration which the individual now enjoys. It will be sufficient for our purpose to notice the general scope of the Swiss law.

The Swiss law of 1880 has been superseded by the law of May 24, 1888. The main provisions of this law are as follows : —

I. The business of forwarding emigrants is subjected to very close supervision. No person can

---

[1] Résumé of the new Italian law in an article by Eugene Schuyler on Italian Immigration, in The Political Science Quarterly, September, 1889.

engage in it without a license from the federal council. Licenses shall be issued only to such persons as furnish proof that they enjoy a good reputation and are in possession of civil rights and honors, are familiar with the business of emigration, and have a fixed domicile in the confederation. A yearly fee of fifty francs is to be paid for a license, and the license may be withdrawn if the holder no longer fulfils the provisions noted above, or transgresses the law, or participates in any colonization scheme against which the federal council has issued a warning. Each agency must deposit security to the amount of 40,000 francs, and further security to the amount of 3,000 francs for each sub-agent appointed. The security can be returned to the depositor only after the lapse of one year from the expiration of the license, and if claims then exist against the agency the security shall stand until these are settled. No agent or sub-agent shall be in the service of, or in any way dependent upon, any railroad or transatlantic steamship company. The names of all licensed agents and sub-agents shall be entered in a book and published in the official gazette. To all other persons announcements pertaining to emigration are prohibited.

II. Agents are forbidden to forward: (1) Persons incapable of labor owing to advanced age, disease, or infirmity, so far as no evidence is forthcoming of adequate maintenance at the place of destination. (2) Minors, or persons under guardianship, unless provided with the written, authenticated consent of the parent or guardian. (3) Persons who after defraying the expenses of the journey would arrive without means at place of destination. (4) Persons forbidden to land by the laws of the country to which they wish to emigrate. (5) Persons who are in possession of no papers showing their place of origin and citizenship. (6) Swiss citizens liable to military duty who are not able to produce evidence that they have returned the equipments which they have received from the state. (7) Parents desiring to leave children, not yet raised, behind them, and to whose emigration the poor authorities have not agreed.

III. There are minute provisions as to the form of contract, the supplies to be furnished the emigrant on his journey both by land and by sea, care for him while at the port of shipment, free medical attendance, decent interment in case of death on the route, insurance of baggage, etc.

IV. Persons or companies desiring to carry out colonization schemes must submit them to the federal council, which has the right to determine whether or not, and under what conditions, parties may be allowed to present them. Agencies, as well as colonization companies, are forbidden to conclude contracts by which they obligate themselves to deliver a certain number of persons either to a shipping company, or to a colonization or other project, or to state governments. The federal council is authorized to prohibit advertisements in public journals, or other publications of any kind calculated to mislead persons desiring to emigrate. The council shall establish a bureau which shall place itself in communication with points of importance in other countries, and shall, when called upon, furnish necessary information, advice, and recommendations to persons desiring to emigrate. The council may, within the limits of the credit granted to it for this purpose, take the necessary measures in order that emigrants may be furnished with advice and assistance at the principal ports of embarkation and debarkation. Swiss consuls are directed to inquire without charge into any complaint made by Swiss emigrants for violations of the conditions guaranteed them, if the complaints are lodged within ninety-six hours after the complainant's arrival; and on demand of the complainant, to draw up a report of the case and transmit a copy thereof to the federal council.[1]

It is not difficult to find justification for such a law as this. It is intended to protect the emigrant who is still a citizen of the state, to prevent the violation

---

[1] Translation of the law on page 113 of reports from consuls appended to the Ford Immigration Committee report.

of international obligations respecting the sending out of undesirable persons, and to stop a migratory movement which has no good cause, but is artificially produced and maintained. It is a preventive rather than a restrictive measure, and need not stand in the way of any really desirable movement of efficient and energetic men to better their condition by seeking a new field for their industrial powers. It will, however, prevent a great deal of suffering and disappointment on the part of the emigrant and dissatisfaction on the part of the country receiving him. It seems to put this important social movement on a common sense basis, where we can watch it and to a certain extent at least guide it, in the interest of the persons and communities concerned. If through these measures the migratory movement becomes less general but more intelligent, it will be a gain to all parties, and not the least so to those countries to which the movement is directed.

The emigrant is an object of care not only to the country which he is forsaking, but even more so to the country he is seeking. Thus the United States early took an interest in the treatment of emigrants on board ship and at the port of landing. The United States has passengers' acts similar in scope to the British and intended to remedy the abuses which had grown up about the business of transporting immigrants. In addition it has made provision for the reception of the immigrant after he has landed at Castle Garden or other place of entry. Mr. Friedrich Kapp[1] has given a vivid account of the sufferings of the emigrant during his voyage and upon landing in New York, previous to the passage of the passengers' acts and the establishment of the board of commissioners of emigration. The vessels were small sailing vessels; the emigrants were crowded into the space between decks which was seldom more than five feet in height and sometimes less, lighted and ventilated only by the hatches which were battened down during bad weather; sometimes the orlop deck below that was also used for passengers. The emigrants were obliged to provide their own food and cook it at the galleys which were insufficient in number for the passengers, so that there was a constant struggle to get to them, and the food was badly cooked. The filth, bad air and insufficient nourishment gave rise to disease and sickness, against which there was no adequate provision for medical treatment. The emigrants were at the mercy of the brutality and greed of the officers and crew of the ship, and often suffered corporal punishment or were put on short allowance of food. The voyage lasted many weeks, sometimes months; the mortality was enormous, often ten and sometimes

[1] Kapp, Immigration and the Commissioners of Emigration of the State of New York. New York, 1870. Chapter 2.

twenty per cent; and those who arrived were either sick, or enfeebled and unable to take care of themselves and quickly became applicants for admission to the hospitals and almshouses of the state.

Many of these evils have been remedied by the substitution of steamships for sailing vessels, by which the voyage is shorter and the space and accommodations more generous. Legislation has also been invoked to protect the immigrant.

The first passengers' act of the United States was passed in 1819. It provided that no ship should carry more than two passengers to every five tons of the ship's burden. The act was not very effective because it did not regulate the relation between the ship's burden and the amount of space devoted to the carrying of passengers. In early times ships were not fitted up especially for the carriage of passengers, but such space as was left after the freight was secured was filled with passengers. Thus a ship of a thousand tons' burden would be entitled to carry four hundred passengers, although only half of the space between decks was given up to their use. The act of 1855 was much more effective, securing sufficient space for each passenger, providing for ventilation, for a plentiful supply of food and for its cooking and distribution. The act of 1882 provides 100 cubic feet of space for each passenger (120 feet if on the lower deck), and contains minute regulations similar to the English act.

But it was through the legislation of the state of New York that the first efficient provision was made for the care of the immigrant. As immigration increased it was found to be imposing a heavy burden on the poor relief of New York city, many of the immigrants entering the almshouse or hospital a few days after their arrival. Accordingly in 1824 the legislature of New York passed an act requiring the master of every ship bringing alien passengers to the port of New York to enter into a bond, in such sum as the mayor or recorder of the city might deem sufficient, not to exceed three hundred dollars for each passenger, to indemnify the city in case any said immigrants or children born of them after importation should become a charge on the city within two years after the date of the bond.[1] An ordinance of the city of New York allowed the master of the ship to escape the execution of the bond by the payment of a sum varying from one to ten dollars for each alien passenger.

These acts, according to Kapp, led to evasions and great abuses. The bonds were often insufficient; when an immigrant became a charge on the city it was difficult to identify him and compel the persons

---

[1] Kapp, Immigration, etc., p. 45.

responsible to pay for him; speculators entered into contracts to secure the captains against further responsibility on the basis of so much a passenger, or even so much a ship, and these speculators availed themselves of every device for evading payment of the bond. Finally they went so far as to establish private almshouses, where the pauper immigrants were cared for at a cheaper rate than in the city almshouses. The most flagrant abuses sprang up in these institutions. The inmates were treated in the harshest and most inhumane manner, and after the two years required by law had expired they were thrown on the county for support. In 1842 a committee of the board of aldermen reported the inefficiency of the bonding system, and recommended that a uniform tax of one dollar be levied on the immigrants for the benefit of the city. They declared that only one-ninth of the immigrants were commuted for by the captains, and that it was difficult to hold the bondsmen to their obligation, so that while during the last three years the number of passengers landed at the port had been 181,615, the city had received only $41,391. That left $140,223 which had gone into the pockets of private individuals, for the shipowners were accustomed to collect one dollar from each immigrant by adding it to the fare.[1] The financial interests of the city demanded a change; while

[1] Kapp, Immigration, etc., p. 50.

the lowest sense of justice could be satisfied with nothing less than that the money collected from the immigrants should be administered for their benefit.

The treatment of the ordinary immigrants was a disgrace to the administrative authorities of New York city and to American civilization. As soon as an emigrant ship reached the port it was boarded by a class of men called "runners," in the employment of boarding-house keepers or of forwarding companies. Disputes between rival runners often led to violence, and the unfortunate immigrant was decoyed, often half-forced, into the boarding-house. There he was charged three or four times the prices he had been promised; if he did not pay, his baggage was held in custody. He was persuaded to buy transportation over particular routes by misrepresentations; he was charged extravagant prices for his ticket; his baggage was falsely weighed; and in every way he was victimized. Helpless, in a strange country, ignorant often of the language, not knowing whom to trust, he was obliged to submit to extortion and went on his way, making place for new victims. The author of the wrong went unpunished because there was no one to make complaint. These evils continued until 1855, when Castle Garden was made the landing-place for all immigrants, and they could there be protected against sharpers.[1]

[1] Kapp, Immigration, etc., chapter 4.

The financial interests of the city and the notorious wrongs perpetrated on the immigrants led finally to an agitation in 1846–47 for a reform of the law. The city council favored the abolition of the bonding system, and the payment of a head-tax to the mayor or comptroller of the city for the purpose of defraying the expenses of poor relief. This would have secured the financial interests of the city. But a number of public-spirited gentlemen believed that the measure did not go far enough to remedy the abuses connected with the treatment of immigrants. They therefore agitated for a different measure, which was finally passed by the legislature and became a law, May 5, 1847. This law established the first Board of Emigration Commissioners of the State of New York. Six commissioners were named in the bill, who were to hold office for two, four, and six years, their successors to be appointed by the governor and to hold office for six years. To these were added as *ex officio* members of the board, the mayor of the city of New York, the mayor of the city of Brooklyn, the president, for the time being, of the Irish Immigration Society, and the president, for the time being, of the German Immigration Society.[1]

This board of commissioners was to have full power of taking charge of all immigrants who should within five years of their landing come on the poor relief of

[1] Kapp, Immigration, etc., chapter 5.

any city or county in the state; it was to have power to remove them from one part of the state to another, or from the state, and to lease or purchase property and erect buildings for the purpose of carrying out the provisions of the act. Money was to be provided by a head-tax of one dollar on each immigrant, which was afterwards increased to two, and later to two and a half dollars. The commissioners were afterwards authorized to lease a pier where all immigrants should be landed and to which other persons should be admitted only by a permit. This was in order to protect the immigrant from extortion. It was not, however, till 1855 that the commissioners succeeded in securing what is known as Castle Garden. There the immigrants are landed and inspected; those who desire to proceed to the interior purchase tickets from the regular railroad agents, and have their baggage weighed and sent free of charge to the depot; those who stay in the city can have their baggage delivered at fixed rates; only boarding-house keepers holding licenses from the mayor and whose houses are subject to inspection and regulation are admitted to the garden to solicit custom; the immigrant has his money exchanged by authorized brokers at posted rates; he is supplied with food according to fixed prices; and every effort is made to protect him against fraud and imposition.[1]

[1] Reports of Commissioners of Emigration of the State of New York.

The enormous increase of immigration after 1847 made it extremely difficult to provide the necessary poorhouses and hospitals for the helpless and infirm among the immigrants. The commissioners at first leased and afterwards acquired by purchase land on Ward's Island, and there established their own hospital. These purchases were continued from time to time until in 1868 they had acquired over 120 acres at a cost of $140,000. The property is said to be worth now from two to three million dollars. The term during which the commissioners were obliged to receive the immigrant was reduced in 1882 from five years to one year after the landing. At the expiration of that time they are turned over to the authorities of the county of New York. In 1888 there were 4,136 persons admitted to the hospital and 202 persons to the insane asylum on Ward's Island.

The work of the Emigration Commissioners of the State of New York has been performed with great fidelity. The board was originally instituted in order to protect the immigrant and secure the community against too heavy a burden for poor relief. There was no intention of restricting immigration. It was considered desirable, and the labors of the board were calculated to facilitate rather than to hinder it. Of late years that feeling has changed, and the demand has arisen that immigration if not to be actually restricted is to be closely watched and undesirable immigrants kept out. With this feeling the board of emigration commissioners of New York has been called upon to do the work of inspection and the enforcement of the regulating acts of Congress. Moreover, as four-fifths of the immigration come through the port of New York, the whole country looks to it for the efficient discharge of this new and onerous duty. It has not been able to meet these demands altogether satisfactorily, partly from the nature of the case and partly from recent legislation. Composed of private citizens serving without pay and busied with their own affairs the commission was well fitted to administer a great charity, while it is not fitted to discharge invidious administrative duties where it would encounter the opposition of powerful moneyed corporations. In addition it has been crippled by legislation and adverse judicial decisions.

In 1876 the imposition of the head-money upon which the board of commissioners was dependent for its financial resources was declared unconstitutional by the Supreme Court of the United States, on the ground that it was a regulation of commerce.[1] The steamship companies refusing to pay the head-money any longer, the board was made dependent on annual grants from the legislature of the state of New

[1] Henderson *vs.* Mayor of New York, etc., 97 U. S. R. 259. The Inman Steamship Co. sued the board for back commutation moneys, but an act of Congress, 1878, legalized the past actions of the commissioners. Report, 1879.

York.[1] A state act of 1881 imposing a tax of one dollar on each immigrant, under the title of an inspection law, was in like manner declared unconstitutional.[2] It was felt to be unjust that the burden of immigration should be borne by the state of New York, when its benefits were enjoyed by the whole nation. If the state of New York did not have the right to impose a tax for the purpose of protecting the immigrants, it was felt that the United States ought either to undertake the duty or at least furnish the money. The commissioners prepared a national act and presented it to Congress year after year, but without success. Finally when Congress passed the act of 1882 forbidding the immigration of paupers, criminals and persons unable to take care of themselves, it provided for the payment of a head-tax of fifty cents on each immigrant. This money was to be paid to the Secretary of the Treasury, who was authorized to enter into contract with any state officers of emigration for the purpose of enforcing the act. The Secretary of the Treasury now contracts with the board of commissioners of emigration of the state of New York for the inspection of immigrants arriving at the port of New York. The act has embarrassed the commissioners in several ways. The secretary refuses to

---

[1] 1877, $200,000; subsequent years $150,000 annually; total amount 1876—1882, $1,000,000.

[2] People vs. Compagnie Générale Transatlantique, 107 U. S. R. 59.

pay out of the tax the rental of Ward's Island or for improvements and permanent repairs on the property there. The commissioners have paid for repairs and insurance by the sale of privileges in Castle Garden, but the money due from this source is also in dispute, the commissioners claiming that it belongs to the state, the secretary that it belongs to the national immigrant fund. In 1888 the Attorney-General decided that the money belonged to the state, but the rental hitherto paid by the United States government for Castle Garden was disallowed.[1] Finally, the commissioners are empowered to inspect immigrants according to the law of 1882, but the decision whether any person shall be sent back or not rests with the collector of the port. In 1888, twenty-eight per cent of those rejected by the commissioners were allowed by the collector to land.

The commissioners have been embarrassed also by the action of the legislature of New York, which in 1883 abolished the board and provided for a new board of three commissioners, one to be appointed by the governor with the advice and consent of the senate, and to have a salary of $6000, the other two to be the president of the Irish and the president of the German Immigration Society. The senate has, however, refused to confirm the governor's appointees, so that the present commissioners are holding over until

---

[1] Report of Commissioners, 1888.

their successors are appointed. They have quarrelled among themselves, two have resigned, and it is often impossible at the present time to get a quorum for the transaction of business.

CHAPTER XI.

CHINESE IMMIGRATION.

No treatment of immigration would be complete without reference to the prohibition of Chinese immigration by the United States and the British colonies in North America and Australia. It would be a difficult and ungrateful task to enter a defence of the brutal treatment of Chinese resident in this country, or even to justify entirely our legislation and diplomacy in regard to their exclusion. Too much of it bears the stamp of demagogic subserviency to the passing demands of the mob. The best way, perhaps, is to acknowledge that our conduct has not been all that it should have been, and to deplore the cases where injury and injustice have been inflicted. On the other hand, the gradual modification of certain notions respecting the efficacy of general "a priori" principles for the practical guidance of a nation may lead us to admit that there is some deeper reason for the exclusion of this foreign element than mere dislike. It is intended here only to trace the course of our legislation, and to point out the particular ground on which the exclusion of the Chinese rests.

It is a matter of common knowledge that during

the greater part of our national life we have been very much influenced by general doctrines concerning the rights of man. Embodied in our Declaration of Independence, reinforced by French philosophy, and commended by the success of democratic institutions among ourselves, the principles of liberty and equality have been insisted upon by us with no little emphasis. The great influx of immigrants having the definite intention of remaining here forced us to the contention that among the rights of man was that of free migration and expatriation. We could take no other position. It was impossible for the thousands of immigrants to retain their old allegiance; and it was undesirable that they should have any less rights, whether at home or abroad, than our own native born citizens. We have already seen how completely we carried out this idea in our naturalization laws and our treaties with foreign powers concerning the right of expatriation. By a resolution of Congress of July 27, 1868, the right of expatriation was declared to be "a natural and inherent right of all people, indispensable to the enjoyment of the rights of life, liberty and the pursuit of happiness"; and, "any declaration, instruction, opinion, order or decision of any officer of the United States which denies, restricts, obstructs or questions the right of expatriation is declared inconsistent with the fundamental principles of the Republic."

That same year a specific application of this doctrine was made in a treaty concluded with China, as follows:

> "The United States of America and the Emperor of China cordially recognize the inherent and inalienable right of man to change his home and allegiance, and also the mutual advantage of the free migration and emigration of their citizens and subjects respectively, from the one country to the other, for the purposes of curiosity, of trade or as permanent residents."[1]

This treaty of 1868 marks the dividing line between two distinct and contradictory policies on the part of the United States in its relations with China and the Chinese. Up to that time our efforts had been directed towards compelling the Chinese to admit Americans to China for the pursuit of trade and commerce. In this contention we placed ourselves on the broad platform of the right of free migration and the duty of international intercourse. Shortly after this declaration we found that the influx of Chinese into this country was causing inconvenience, and we immediately turned our backs on the principle of freedom of migration, and passed laws excluding the Chinese as effectually as they had ever excluded foreigners.

Our political relations with China date back to the year 1844, when Caleb Cushing negotiated the first treaty between the United States and that country.

[1] Burlingame Treaty, Article V. Concluded July 28, 1868.

That treaty, like all subsequent ones, had for its object, so far as the United States was concerned, two things. One was the protection of the lives and property of American citizens in China; the other was the securing of privileges of trade and commerce. For the first object, the Chinese government granted extra-territorial consular jurisdiction to the United States; that is, "citizens of the United States who may commit any crime in China shall be subject to be tried and punished only by the consul, or other public functionary of the United States, thereto authorized, according to the laws of the United States." In regard to the other point, the Chinese consented that the Americans should be admitted to five ports for the purposes of trade; but this right was narrowly restricted.

The United States did not take any part in the Chinese war of 1858, but American diplomatic representatives followed in the wake of English and French armies and participated in the advantages of the Chinese discomfiture. The result was the negotiation of the Reed treaty of 1858 commonly known as the treaty of Tient-tsin. By it the number of ports opened to commerce was increased to seven (subsequently still further increased to eleven); the extra-territorial jurisdiction of the consuls was continued; the exercise of the Christian religion was permitted; Chinese pirates might be seized by American men-of-war; tonnage and customs duties were regulated; the United States minister was to be allowed to visit Pekin once a year and to reside there as soon as that privilege was granted to the minister of any foreign power; and finally, Americans were always to enjoy the same rights as the citizens of the most favored nation.

Nothing was said in these treaties about the rights of Chinese trading or residing in the United States. It is said that no provision was necessary, for the Chinese came here under exactly the same conditions as the citizens of any other nation and enjoyed exactly the same privileges. Under our laws at that time they were allowed to come and go freely, to engage in any occupation they pleased; and if they committed crimes they were subject to the jurisdiction of our courts.

The treaty of 1868, which was negotiated by Anson Burlingame at the head of a Chinese embassy visiting this country, went still further in the direction of opening up China to the citizens of the United States. The general declaration (quoted above) of the inherent right of migration was made, coupled with the declaration that any involuntary emigration was to be reprobated; and engaging in such involuntary emigration was to be made a penal offence for the subjects of either power. This clause was directed against the coolie traffic. The provisions of the treaty of 1858 protecting Christian citizens of the

United States and Chinese converts from persecution in China, were renewed and made reciprocal in behalf of Chinese living in the United States who were to have freedom of religious worship and sepulture for their dead. Citizens of either country were to have and enjoy all the privileges of educational institutions under the control of the other country. Finally it was stipulated that:

"Citizens of the United States visiting or residing in China shall enjoy the same privileges, immunities and exemptions in respect to travel or residence as may there be enjoyed by the citizens or subjects of the most favored nation. And, reciprocally, Chinese subjects visiting or residing in the United States, shall enjoy the same privileges, immunities and exemptions in respect to travel or residence as may there be enjoyed by the citizens or subjects of the most favored nation. But nothing herein contained shall be held to confer naturalization upon citizens of the United States in China, nor upon the subjects of China in the United States." Article VII.

Such was the famous Burlingame treaty of 1868. The Chinese embassy was received with most marked attentions in its journey through the United States, at San Francisco, at New York and at Washington. The treaty was hailed with delight as the final opening up of China to the commerce and civilization of the West. Merchants expected a great extension of commerce between China and the Pacific coast; and the Christian churches in America considered that a great obstacle to missionary effort in China had been removed.

As a matter of fact it does not appear that the Burlingame treaty changed the actual condition of things very much. The privileges granted to American citizens in China in regard to trade and religion were precisely those granted in the treaty of 1858. China promised then to treat American citizens in the same way that she treated the subjects of the most favored nation. She promised to do no more now. The reciprocal privileges granted to the Chinese of free exercise of their religion here and to Americans of free entrance to the educational institutions of China were of no practical value, because one was already enjoyed and the other would hardly be desired. The position of the Chinese here was precisely that which they had always shared with other foreigners. The only privilege which they had not enjoyed or of which their enjoyment was doubtful (namely, of naturalization) was expressly withheld by the treaty.

There was one thing, however, which made the treaty in later years and with the change in sentiment towards the Chinese full of embarrassment for the United States. That was the express declaration that the right of migration is inalienable and the express promise that "the subjects of China shall enjoy the same privileges, immunities and exemptions in respect to travel and residence as may be enjoyed by the citizens or subjects of the most favored nation." Thereby that which, on our part, had been merely a tacit understanding or the actually existing condition of things became an express treaty stipulation, requiring formal negotiation to modify, or express statute to over-ride, recourse to either of which might put in jeopardy the privileges accorded under the same treaty to American citizens in China. We thereby expressly committed ourselves, and under the most solemn circumstances, to principles which a few years later we flatly repudiated.

It has been said in extenuation of our later conduct, and it was said even at the time, that the treaty of 1868 and the preceding treaties did not secure any real reciprocity; that while the Chinese under the most favored nation clause were allowed to travel and settle in all parts of the United States and enjoy the same privileges in regard to trade and protection to life and property as the people of the United States, Americans in China were still restricted to certain specified seaports, that they had no access to the interior and that they did not enjoy the same rights in China that the Chinese enjoyed in America. The answer of course is that Americans enjoyed the rights which were stipulated for in the treaty, namely, the same privileges, immunities and exemptions as were enjoyed by the citizens or subjects of the most favored nation. That was all that China agreed to give and all probably in the condition of things there that she could give. At any rate it was what we stipulated for and what we received in return for giving to Chinamen the privileges of the most favored nation here, except that of naturalization. If we look at the question of reciprocity in that light, China might also say that the treaty was not reciprocal, for instance in the matter of consular jurisdiction. For if an American committed a crime in China he was tried by his own consul; while if a Chinaman committed a crime in America he was tried by the American courts and according to American law. It is evident that in 1868 we committed ourselves, as far as solemn treaty obligations could commit us, to treating the Chinese in America precisely (always excepting naturalization) as we treated foreigners of other nationalities.

From this high plane of ideal politics we quickly descended. In 1870 on the revision of the naturalization laws, a proposition[1] in the Senate to insert the words "or persons born in the Chinese empire" after the words "aliens of African nativity and to persons of African descent" was easily negatived. In 1878, Judge Sawyer, in the circuit court of the United States, decided that a Chinaman could not be naturalized as a citizen of the United States.[2] The

[1] By Senator Trumbull, July 4.
[2] 5 Sawyer, 155, quoted by Wharton, Int. Law Digest, § 197.

anti-Chinese feeling, which had already existed for some time on the Pacific coast, entered into national politics and the leaders of the two parties pandered to it for the purpose of securing the vote of those states. In 1876 both parties inserted an anti-Chinese plank in their platforms, and a special joint committee of the Senate and the House of Representatives proceeded to the Pacific coast to investigate the question on the spot, and formulated a report painting the evils of Chinese immigration in the strongest and blackest colors and demanding immediate legislation. In order to understand the rapid culmination of this feeling against the Chinese which resulted in the report of 1876 and the subsequent legislation, it will be necessary to turn for a moment to the history of Chinese immigration into California and the treatment the Chinese had there received.

Chinese immigration began soon after the discovery of the gold fields, but for the first few years there are no exact statistics of the arrivals and departures. From 1848 to 1852 the number is estimated to have been 10,000 for the four years.[1] In 1852 the number of arrivals was 20,026 and of departures 1768. In 1853 the arrivals were 4270, but the departures were 4421, that is, in excess of the arrivals. In 1854 the arrivals were 16,084 and the departures 2330. During the next fifteen years the

[1] Report of Committee on Chinese Immigration, 1876, p. 1196.

arrivals were only a few thousand per annum, never more than 8424, and the annual departures were three or four thousand so that the annual increase was not very great; in some years in fact there was an excess of departures over arrivals. In 1868 the arrivals were 11,085 and the net gain was 6876. In 1868 the net gain was 10,098, and down to 1876 the excess of arrivals over departures was never more than 11,000 per annum and often less than that number. From 1848 to 1876, a period of nearly thirty years, the total arrivals were estimated at 233,136 and the departures at 93,273, leaving a net gain of 139,863. Deducting a loss by mortality of two per cent per annum (which is the mortality of the white population) making 25,900, there was estimated to be in the United States in 1876 about 114,000 Chinese. This number was subsequently proven to have been exaggerated. The census of 1880 showed only 105,000 Chinese here.

The Chinese were at first regarded without aversion by the other immigrants into California. Their peculiarities of dress, their inoffensive manners and general defencelessness soon brought upon them abuse and persecution from the rough elements gathered in the mining camps. The robbery or murder of a Chinaman was seldom avenged. Immigrants of other nationalities, quick to feel their supposed superiority to the "heathen Chinee," expressed it by stoning him upon the streets, by mobbing him in his house, and by general abuse and violence. His untiring industry and perseverance made him successful in the placer mines, the Chinaman often working over places abandoned by the white miner; and envy and ill-will soon attacked him as a competitor with white labor. As he subsequently engaged in work on the railroad, on the farm, as domestic servant, and finally even in certain manufactures, his labor was denounced as superseding that of the white man, and the question of Chinese immigration became a labor question to which the statesmen of California almost immediately succumbed. The Chinaman had no vote, and hence could have no influence in politics.

Popular feeling against the Chinaman soon expressed itself in state legislation and city ordinances, directed specifically or indirectly against him. An act of the California legislature in 1855 imposed a tax of $55 on every Chinese immigrant. A subsequent act (1858) prohibited all persons of the Chinese or Mongolian races from entering the state or landing at any port thereof, unless driven on shore by stress of weather or unavoidable accident, in which case they should immediately be re-shipped. An act was passed in 1862 providing that every Mongolian over eighteen years of age should pay a monthly capitation tax of $2.50, except those engaged in the production and manufacture of sugar, rice, coffee and tea. All of these acts were declared unconstitutional by the Supreme Court of California.[1] In 1861 there was passed the act imposing a tax on foreign miners. It read as follows:

"No person unless he is a citizen of the United States, or shall have declared his intention to become such (California Indians excepted), shall be allowed to take or extract gold, silver, or other metals from the mines of this state, or hold a mining claim therein, unless he shall have a license therefor of $4 per month."[2]

This act was levelled nominally against all foreigners, but the universal testimony is that it was enforced only against the Chinese. At any rate, they were the only ones who could not escape it, for they were not allowed to become naturalized. The tax collectors were often prejudiced men, who used the authority conferred upon them in the most violent manner. The committee of the California legislature which inquired into the Chinese question in 1862 declared that eighty-eight cases had been reported to them where Chinamen had been murdered by white people, eleven of whom were known to have been murdered by collectors of the foreign miner's license tax — sworn officers of the law. But two of the murderers had been convicted and hanged.[3]

---

[1] Report on Chinese Immigration, p. 477.

[2] This tax dates back to 1853, and was modified at different times, varying from $4 to $6 and to $20.

[3] Seward, Chinese Immigration, p. 37 ff.

In like manner a number of city ordinances were passed for the purpose of reaching the Chinese indirectly. Thus, San Francisco had a laundry ordinance imposing a license fee as follows: On laundries using a one-horse vehicle, $2 per quarter; two horses, $4 per quarter; no vehicle, $15 per quarter. The Chinese laundries commonly used no vehicle. Men who sold vegetables on the street from door to door were required to pay a fee of $2 if they drove a wagon, of $10 if they went on foot. The so-called "queue ordinance" provided that every person convicted for any criminal offence should have his hair cut to a length of one inch from his head. This was especially felt by the Chinaman, to whom the loss of his queue was a lasting disgrace. The "cubic air ordinance" required that no person should let or hire any tenement house where the capacity of the rooms was less than five hundred cubic feet for every person sleeping there. This ordinance was enforced only against the Chinese. Of these petty persecutions all that even Senator Sargent could say was: "That [the laundry ordinance] was one of the methods this city and state have tried, to rid themselves of this great plague, before appealing to Congress. It may appear ridiculous, cutting off queues, etc., but they resort to those things before resorting to violence."[1]

By an act of legislature of 1863 it was provided

[1] Report on Chinese Immigration, p. 479.

that Chinese and Mongolians should not be witnesses in an action or proceeding wherein a white person was party. It was afterwards repealed.[1]

The efforts of the California legislature to stop Chinese immigration were rendered futile by the decisions of the United States courts. These decisions prevented any discrimination against the Chinese by name because it would be a violation of treaty obligations. On the other hand, the prohibition or even regulation of immigration was held to be a regulation of commerce, and hence to belong exclusively to Congress. This was clearly shown by the decision of the Supreme Court of the United States on the constitutionality of that part of the political code of California which gave the commissioner of immigration power to exclude from the state lunatics, idiots, deaf and dumb persons, cripples, lewd and debauched women, etc. The aim of the statute was to exclude Chinese prostitutes. The court decided, however, that the state could not confer upon an officer the power of going on board a ship and designating such persons as he might deem to come within the statute and preventing their landing. Such power involved international relations, and belonged to Congress alone.[2]

Met at every turn by the adverse decisions of the

---

[1] Report on Chinese Immigration, p. 478.
[2] Chy Lung vs. J. H. Freeman et al., 92 U. S. Reports.

courts, the Californians finally decided to appeal to Congress for national action to put a stop to Chinese immigration. The legislature authorized the municipality of San Francisco to appropriate the sum of five thousand dollars to pay the expenses of a delegation to Washington to "solicit such action on the part of the Federal government as should modify the Burlingame treaty, so as to prevent the immigration of certain classes of Chinese under its provisions, whose arrival in our midst is detrimental to the moral and material interests of our own people."

The testimony collected by the Congressional committee which was sent in response to this demand covers every phase of the Chinese question, and is of value to-day as showing at least the way in which the Chinese were regarded by the various classes of people in California. Much of the evidence is colored by prejudice, some of it is economically and politically absurd, and there is no general agreement among the witnesses; but still we can reach some conclusions.

The opponents of the Chinese asserted that there was danger of the white population of California becoming outnumbered by the Chinese; that they came here under contract, in other words as coolies or a servile class; that they were subject to the jurisdiction of organized companies which directed their movements, settled disputes among them, and even had power of life and death, which they exercised by assassination; that Chinese cheap labor deprived white labor of employment, lowered wages, and kept white immigrants from coming to the state; that the Chinese were loathsome in their habits, and the filth of their dwellings endangered the health of the city; that they were vile in their morals, and spread prostitution, gambling and opium habits; that they did not assimilate with the whites, and never could become an integral and homogeneous part of the population.

The evidence shows, in my opinion, that many of these assertions are entirely too sweeping. The number of Chinese in the state (which was asserted by their accusers to be from 150,000 to 175,000) was grossly exaggerated, as was shown by the census of 1880. They failed entirely to prove the existence of any such thing as the coolie traffic. There are organizations known as the "six companies," and their exact function was not discovered, but they seem to be associations of men from the same province for mutual assistance and protection. It was not proven, however, that the companies exercise any absolute authority over the Chinese, or inflict punishments upon them for disobedience to their orders. The personal habits of the Chinese, as far as their dwellings are concerned, seem to be filthy in the extreme, but it did not appear that the municipal government had taken any steps to improve the condition of the Chinese quarter. They did not seem to have more disease or greater mortality than is usual among people of the working classes. Their habits of personal cleanliness compare favorably with those of laborers of other nationalities. As far as criminality is concerned, they are peaceable, law abiding, never drunk, and are represented in the statistics of the prisons by less than their proportionate number. They are inveterate gamblers. They are also opium smokers; which latter vice, however, seems to be less of a public nuisance than drunkenness, for it simply stupefies the victim instead of exciting him. Chinese prostitution is a real evil, and women are brought from China for that especial purpose, and bound under contract. It is an evil incident to the peculiar character of the immigration which consists of adult males unaccompanied by their families. It is a question how far it can be controlled either by consular inspection before the women are allowed to leave China or by municipal measures here. The real evil consists in the presence of that great number of men without their families.

Passing by these considerations, which do not seem to involve any grave national dangers, we come to the more serious questions of the economic effect of Chinese immigration and of their assimilation with our institutions and civilization. The real excuse for their exclusion, if there be any, is to be sought under one of these two categories.

On the question of the economic effect of the presence of the Chinese the testimony is one mass of hopeless confusion. Most of the witnesses had no economic notions at all, or, if they had any, they were of the most rudimentary and popular kind. To many of them the very presence of a Chinaman in any productive employment seemed conclusive evidence that he displaced a white man; that he would work for low wages made him a direct competitor with the Caucasian; and that he sent his savings back to China constituted a dead loss to the state. They forgot that in a new state there might be room for both Mongolian and White; that the presence of one body of laborers often creates a demand for other kinds of labor; and that the wealth produced by the Chinaman remained in the state, whatever he might do with his surplus wages. There doubtless comes a time when an excessive supply of labor introduces competition among the laborers and lowers wages. But there was little effort on the part of witnesses, and none at all in the report of the committee, to determine whether that time had arrived in the case of California.

The general drift of the testimony (and even the opponents of the Chinese did not deny it) was that the Chinaman up to that time had been extremely useful in developing the resources of the state. He had made an excellent laborer in the mines, where he had shown himself equal to the most exhausting kinds of work. The builders of the Pacific railroads had employed him when they could not find an adequate supply of white labor. He had reclaimed thousands of acres of "tule" (*i.e.* marsh) lands, where the white laborer could not work on account of malaria. The wheat harvests of the state could not have been gathered had it not been for the Chinese coming to the assistance of the farmers. All through the state he was employed as a domestic servant, and in many places, especially in the rural districts, no other house servants could be obtained. In some few manufacturing industries he had been introduced, but it was probable that these industries could never have been established in California had it not been for the cheap labor of the Chinese. In regard to competition with white labor, it would appear that where every kind of labor was so scarce there need have been no competition, for there was employment for all; still further, that, while the Chinese took the drudgery, the whites assumed the places of skilled laborers and bosses; for instance, that the heads of the section gangs on the railroads and in the mines were invariably whites; that the teamsters on the farms were always whites, the Chinese not being skilful in handling horses; and that there were no Chinese blacksmiths, carpenters, masons, bricklayers, etc. It appeared, therefore, that Chinese labor had been of great benefit to California, and not only to the employers of labor, but to all classes of the community, for it had furnished that substratum of rough labor upon which all successful industry must be built. It is unnecessary to discuss here the question how long such labor will be necessary and useful for the state of California. From the purely economic standpoint it is probable that for a long time to come it will be advantageous for the development of the state.

The one serious charge that was substantiated against the desirability of Chinese immigration was that they do not assimilate with us. They come here with the single object of making money and then returning to China. They have no intention of becoming permanent residents, and no desire to adopt our customs and habits of life. The most earnest defenders of the Chinese could not prove that during thirty years of contact our civilization had made any impress upon them. Our effort to christianize them has, with a few exceptions, been an entire failure. They have shown no desire to become acquainted with our political institutions, or to take part in political life. It may be contended that we have refused to admit them to political life, and that the treatment they have received at our hands has not been such as to excite admiration of our civilization. But the very tenacity with which, notwithstanding all this persecution, they have clung to peculiarities of costume and living, causing them to be singled out for abuse, shows that they are singularly conservative in their ideas. The whole history of the intercourse between China and the Western powers has exemplified the fact that, with their four thousand years of civilization behind them, they are imbued with a thorough contempt for the mushroom growths of European life. They feel no sense of inferiority, and hence no desire for change.

In short, without committing ourselves to the ethnological vagaries of the Californian philosophers who assured the committee that the Chinese did not belong to the same species of the *genus homo* as the whites, and that a cross between the two would be infertile,[1] we may say that we have to do with a race which in tenacious adherence to its own culture seems equal to our own. The question of receiving them, therefore, assumes an entirely different aspect from that of receiving immigrants from Europe. The latter blend with the native stock, and all become one people. The Chinese remain isolated, and constitute an alien element in the midst of us. There are but two solutions to such a problem as their coming presents. If they are less in numbers than

---

[1] Judge Hastings, Testimony, p. 586.

we, they remain an inferior class, doing our drudgery, but enjoying none of the rights and performing none of the duties of citizenship. Such a solution is abhorrent to the principles of democracy and incompatible with the maintenance of our institutions. The other solution is that they shall come in such numbers as to overwhelm our civilization, or at least give rise to continual race conflicts in certain parts of our continent. The interests of civilization forbid the opening of even the possibility of such a conflict.[1]

The real question involved in Chinese immigration, therefore, was whether they were likely to come in such numbers as to prove an inconvenience to our civilization. Even Seward, the zealous defender of the Chinese, acknowledges that if there were danger of their coming *en masse* it would be well to protect ourselves.[2] The question is involved in obscurity. The population of China certainly numbers hundreds of millions, and their fertility is enormous. So long as the economic advantages which have already attracted them to this country remain, one cannot see why they should not continue to come, and in increasing masses, as the facilities of transportation improve. Seward maintains that they are a con-

[1] See an excellent article by M. J. Dee in The North American Review, vol. 126, p. 506, 1878.
[2] See also Senator Hamlin, who opposed so vigorously the exclusion bill of 1879. Senate Debates, Feb. 14, 1879.

servative race, and that there is no danger of any such influx. However that may be, the problem was one where we could easily have guarded ourselves against danger by wise negotiation and a friendly understanding with the government of China, which had not the slightest inclination to encourage the emigration of its subjects. We return now to our actual legislation on the subject.

The report of the committee of 1876 was violently denunciatory of the Chinese, and regarded all the statements of their adversaries as fully proven. It admitted that there were some respectable people who defended them, but insinuated that these people were either capitalists who profited by their cheap labor, or clergymen who considered it a religious duty to admit the Chinese in order to christianize them. The report closed as follows:

"The committee recommend that measures be taken by the executive looking toward a modification of the existing treaty with China, confining it to strictly commercial purposes; and that Congress legislate to restrain the great influx of Asiatics to this country. It is not believed that either of these measures would be looked upon with disfavor by the Chinese government. Whether this is so or not, a duty is owing to the Pacific states and territories, which are suffering under a terrible scourge, but are patiently [?] waiting for relief from Congress."

Owing to the excitement caused by the dispute over the presidential election of 1876, no action was taken on the report of the committee. The question did not sleep long. On January 25, 1878, Mr. Willis, from the House committee on Education and Labor, presented a report denouncing Chinese immigration in the strongest terms, and recommending that correspondence be opened with China and Great Britain with a view to putting a stop to it. On January 29, 1879, Mr. Willis again presented a special report, which dealt with three points only: 1st. Can Congress repeal a treaty? 2d. Previous efforts at relief. 3d. Restrictive measures necessary.[1] A bill was at the same time introduced into the House restricting immigration from China to fifteen persons upon any one vessel. Extended debates followed, both in the House and the Senate. The latter are particularly interesting, for the Senate is the treaty-making power, and it is natural to suppose that it would be sensitive about legislation directly abrogating treaty stipulations which it had itself entered into. In the Senate we find only one member, the aged Senator Hamlin of Maine, still standing on the basis of free immigration as a natural right of man and one of the foundation doctrines of the republic. Mr. Hamlin said: "I believe in principles coeval with the foundation of government, that this country is the 'home of the free,' where the outcast of every nation, where the child of every creed and of every clime could

---

[1] Quoted by Seward, p. 299.

breathe our free air and participate in our free institutions." [1]

Senator Matthews of Ohio opposed the bill vigorously because it was a violation of the treaty of 1868, and he believed that we ought first to seek to modify that treaty by diplomatic negotiations. Mr. Blaine tried to evade this point by declaring that China had already broken the provision of the treaty prohibiting the coolie traffic, — a statement for which we are unable to find any evidence in the testimony offered before the committee of 1876. Mr. Sargent of California argued that Congress had the power to abrogate a treaty, although he admitted that it ought not to be done except in an emergency. He tried to prove that Great Britain had contravened her treaty of 1858 with China by laws forbidding the entrance of Chinese into Australian colonies. He finally repeated the old arguments about the dangers of Chinese immigration into California.

The question seems to have gotten into practical politics again, for the bill passed the House by an overwhelming vote and the Senate by a vote of thirty-nine against twenty-seven. It was vetoed by President Hayes on the ground that it was such a violation of the treaty of 1868 as would relieve China from her obligations and expose our citizens in China to the consequences of this abrogation of their treaty

[1] Senate, Feb. 15, 1879.

protection. We were thus saved from the disgrace of breaking a solemn treaty, but in a way that was not very flattering to China.

The executive hastened to comply with the wish of the representatives of the people that the treaty of 1868 should be modified, and a commission was sent in 1880 to China for that purpose. The Chinese proved to be shrewd negotiators, and showed that they were not unconversant with the condition of things in the United States.[1] To the intimation of the American commissioners that a modification of the Burlingame treaty was desirable, they replied: That there was no compulsory emigration from China to the United States; that China rejoiced in the freedom which her subjects enjoyed in America; they also quoted a declaration of Senator Morton, that the constitution declared that all peoples might come to the United States without let or hindrance; and declared that the Chinese in America had added greatly to the wealth of this country. They said still further, that the previous minister, Mr. Seward, had proposed a modification of the treaty for the purpose of prohibiting the emigration of four classes of persons; viz., coolies, prostitutes, criminals and diseased persons. They were quite willing to consider such a proposition, "provided always that such negotiation shall not be contrary to the stipulations of the Burlingame treaty."

[1] For negotiations, see Foreign Relations of U. S., 1880, China.

This unexpected attitude of the Chinese negotiators, together with certain insinuations on their part that the Chinese agitation was simply a concession to practical politics in America, compelled the American commissioners to call them to order quite sharply, by saying that such an insinuation was an insult to the government of the United States, that the recall of Mr. Seward and the sending of the present commission was intimation enough that the modification proposed was not satisfactory; and they finally submitted articles by which the United States government should be allowed to limit, suspend, or prohibit the immigration of Chinese laborers, whenever it saw fit. The measure was not to include persons coming for trade, teaching, travel, study or curiosity.

The Chinese negotiators refused to acquiesce in absolute prohibition; desired that the restrictions should apply to the state of California only; that the term laborer should not include artisans; and that the regulative measures should be submitted to the Chinese minister at Washington for his approval. The last three suggestions the Americans declared to be impossible; but they agreed to drop the word prohibit, and the clause was modified so as to read: "The government of the United States may regulate, limit or suspend such coming or residence, but may not absolutely prohibit it." It was still further agreed that the limitation or suspension should be reasonable, and should apply only to Chinese going to the United States as laborers, other classes being exempt; that the exempt classes and Chinese laborers then in the United States should be allowed to come and go of their own free will and accord; and finally, that "if Chinese laborers or Chinese of any other class now either permanently or temporarily residing in the United States, meet with ill treatment at the hands of any other persons, the government of the United States will exert all of its power to devise measures for their protection, and to secure to them the same rights, privileges, immunities and exemptions as may be enjoyed by the citizens or subjects of the most favored nation, and to which they are entitled by this treaty."

Such was the treaty of 1880. Congress exercised the power therein conferred by the act of May 6, 1882, suspending the immigration of Chinese laborers for the period of ten years.[1] Provision was made however that the act should not apply " to Chinese laborers who were in the United States on the seventeenth day of November, 1880, or who shall have come into the same before the expiration of ninety days next after the passage of this act." If

---

[1] A previous act suspending the immigration of Chinese laborers for twenty years had been vetoed by President Arthur on the ground that it amounted to prohibition.

they desired to leave the country they should receive a certificate from the custom-house officials, on presentation of which they should be allowed re-entry. An act of 1884 made this certificate sole evidence of the fact that a Chinaman had been a resident of this country, it having been found that the courts were crowded with Chinese who wished to prove by parole evidence that they had been residents here before 1882, and the sanctity of an oath not being regarded very highly by the Chinese. The act of 1882 also forbade the naturalization of Chinese by any federal or state court. It declared that the term "laborer" meant both skilled and unskilled laborers and those engaged in mining.

We seemed thus by the treaty of 1880 and the acts in pursuance thereof to have worked ourselves into a position where any possible danger from Chinese immigration would be averted. The number of Chinese laborers was to be absolutely restricted to those already here and, of course, would be constantly diminished by deaths and removals. The act of 1884 was carried out with extreme harshness and gave rise to many cases of individual hardship. For instance, a Chinese laborer who was here in 1880, but departed before the act of 1882 requiring a certificate had been passed, was refused admission on his return on the ground that he had no certificate, which by the act of 1884 was made an indispensable condition of re-admission. Relief was given in his case by the decision of the Supreme Court that the act of Congress should not be interpreted as demanding a condition impossible of fulfilment, and that, although Congress has the power to abrogate treaties by legislative action, yet such power will not be deemed to have been exercised if any other interpretation of the statute is possible.[1] Another hardship was that the statute of 1884 required that even the exempt classes of Chinese coming to the United States should present a certificate issued by Chinese officials if they came from China, or by the officials of other powers if they were subjects of such powers. A Chinese merchant came from Hong-Kong where there was no Chinese official and was refused admission under the act of 1884, although the treaty of 1880 said expressly that restrictions should not apply to merchants.[2]

Still further, notwithstanding all the concessions of the Chinese government in regard to further immigration, the Chinese in America were not treated any better than before. In September, 1885, the Chinese mining laborers in Rock Springs, Wyoming Territory, on refusing to join in a strike were set upon by the whites, twenty-eight were murdered outright, fifteen were wounded, and many others

[1] Chew Heong vs. U. S., 112 U. S. R. 536.
[2] President Cleveland, special message of April 6, 1886.

driven from their homes, while their property to the value of upwards of $147,000 was either destroyed or pillaged by the rioters. The legal investigation by the local officer of the law was a mere travesty of justice.[1] Other outrages followed in Washington Territory. The Chinese minister at Washington appealed for redress on the basis of that article in the treaty of 1880 in which the United States government promised to exert all its power to devise measures for the protection of Chinese who were ill-treated and secure to them the same rights as those enjoyed by the citizens of the most favored nation. He was rewarded by a long disquisition from the Secretary of State on the division of powers in the governmental system of the United States, which puts the preservation of order into the hands of the local authorities, and the declaration that the Chinese enjoyed the same rights as the citizens of any other country when they were injured in person or property, — that is, to sue in the courts. The United States government could not interfere with the local authorities, even in a territory. All this is very true, only one may ask what the United States government intended by the article which it had inserted in the treaty of 1880. The President in successive messages deprecated the Chinese outrages

---

[2] Wharton, Int. Law Digest, vol. 1, p. 475. Secretary of State to Chinese minister.

and recommended that Congress out of its bounty indemnify the sufferers. The sum of $147,000 was appropriated in 1887 for the Rock Springs victims and a further sum of $276,000 was agreed upon in the abortive treaty of 1888.¹ All through these years the outrages continued and the Chinese minister in 1888 sent to our State department a list of forty Chinamen who had been murdered, and up to that time not one of the murderers had been brought to justice.² Payments of money were the only satisfaction which China ever received from this Christian country for outrages disgraceful to our civilization, while she was obliged to give strict account for every offence committed against Christian missionaries in China who were constantly getting themselves into trouble by overstepping the limits fixed by treaty stipulations.

In 1886 the Chinese government announced to the United States minister at Pekin that China of her own accord proposed to establish a system of strict and absolute prohibition, under heavy penalties, of her laborers coming to the United States, and likewise to prohibit the return to the United States of any laborer who had at any time gone back to China "in order that the Chinese laborers may gradually be reduced in number and causes of dan-

---

¹ Foreign Relations, 1888, p. 311.
² *Ibid.* p. 391.

ger averted and lives preserved.[1] We were only too glad to enter into such arrangements and after some negotiations, in which China again attempted (but in vain) to read some meaning into the clause, taken from the treaty of 1880, by which the United States government promised to exert all its power to protect the Chinese already here against ill-treatment, articles were agreed upon between the negotiators. The immigration of Chinese laborers was absolutely prohibited for twenty years; but any Chinese laborer having lawful wife, child, or parent, or property to the amount of $1000 in the United States should be allowed to go out of this country and come back on condition of his obtaining a certificate from the collector of customs and returning within one year. This measure seemed drastic enough, but in order to be perfectly sure, the Senate added two amendments by which the prohibition was expressly extended "to the return of Chinese laborers who are not now in the United States, whether holding certificates under existing laws or not," and the production of a certificate was made absolutely necessary for re-admission. So anxious were we to prevent the return even of those who we had said might return! The Chinese minister received the additional amendments with the remark that they did not materially alter the

[1] Message of President Cleveland, Oct. 1, 1888. Foreign Relations, 1888, p. 357.

treaty, showing that he had expected the harshest interpretation of it as a matter of course, and the treaty was sent on to China for ratification. This was in May, 1888.

The government of the United States confidently expected that China would ratify the treaty and hoped to display it as a master stroke for the satisfaction of the people of the Pacific slope. In China there was unaccountable delay. It seemed that China desired to lessen the term of twenty years, and to gain for Chinese laborers having property less than $1000 in value the right to return. The Congress of the United States grew impatient. A bill was passed for the exclusion of the Chinese, to go into effect as soon as the treaty was ratified, and this measure was signed by the President. Finally the report came by way of England that the Chinese government had rejected the treaty. The politicians in Congress saw their way open to embarrass the Administration and do a good stroke of business, and passed a bill absolutely prohibiting the coming of Chinese laborers to the United States. The State department telegraphed to China to know whether the Chinese government would ratify the treaty or not, and a decision was demanded within forty-eight hours. In the meantime the Chinese ministers had been offended by the report that the House of Representatives had already passed a bill of exclusion, and to the categorical demand of the United States minister they returned answer that the treaty needed further consideration. The President thereupon signed the bill which had been passed by both houses. It is so brutally direct and frank that we give it in full :

"*Be it enacted by the Senate and House of Representatives of the United States of America in Congress assembled*, That from and after the passage of this act, it shall be unlawful for any Chinese laborer who shall at any time heretofore have been, or who may now or hereafter be, a resident within the United States, and who shall have departed, or shall depart, therefrom, and shall not have returned before the passage of this act, to return to, or remain in, the United States.

"SEC. 2. That no certificates of identity provided for in the fourth and fifth sections of the act to which this is a supplement shall hereafter be issued; and every certificate heretofore issued in pursuance thereof, is hereby declared void and of no effect, and the Chinese laborer claiming admission by virtue thereof shall not be permitted to enter the United States.

"SEC. 3. That all the duties prescribed, liabilities, penalties and forfeitures imposed, and the powers conferred by the second, tenth, eleventh and twelfth sections of the act to which this is a supplement are hereby extended and made applicable to the provisions of this act.

"SEC. 4. That all such part or parts of the act to which this is a supplement as are inconsistent herewith are hereby repealed.

"Approved, October 1, 1888."

The President in a message accompanying his approval of the bill declared that the Chinese government in delaying the ratification of the treaty had violated its pledges, and that the demand for further consideration meant an indefinite postponement of the objects that we had in view. While approving the bill the President mildly suggested that it ought not to apply to Chinese already on their way hither, and that the Chinese indemnity money which had been agreed upon in the treaty ought still, out of the "spirit of humanity befitting our nation," to be paid.[1]

The Chinese question has reached the same acute stage in the British colonies that it has in the United States. For many years the Chinese laborers in Australia have been viewed with dislike and jealousy. The same accusations have been brought against them as in California, and for many years the colonial governments have imposed a heavy head-tax on their arrival. Their number has increased until now there are from 43,000 to 45,000 Chinese in Australia. Matters were brought to a crisis by the news that the United States had concluded an exclusion-treaty with China, and a conference was called of the various colonial governments in which it was proposed that the number of Chinese immigrants should be limited to one for every 500 tons of a vessel's burden.[2] The Chinese

---

[1] Foreign Affairs, 1888, p. 356.
[2] See Correspondence relating to Chinese Immigration into the Australian Colonies, 1888.

minister in London protested against this invidious treatment of his countrymen, and Lord Salisbury appealed to the colonies to be patient until a treaty could be concluded with the Chinese government similar to the one which it was supposed would be ratified with the United States. It appears, however, that the restrictive acts are still in force, and in some colonies, British Columbia, for example, they are more severe than any that had ever been enforced in the United States up to the act of 1888. The rejection of the American treaty by China, which was said to be due to Chinese popular opinion, was a severe blow to Lord Salisbury's hope that the matter might be adjusted by negotiation, and no satisfactory arrangement has as yet been reached.

Such is the *status* of the Chinese question at the present time. The Scott bill of 1888 has been declared constitutional by the Supreme Court of the United States, although it over-rides the treaty of 1880, and inflicts hardships on many individuals.[1] The court has declared that the right of a country to exclude aliens from its territory is necessary to its independence, and that any permission it may have given to aliens to come here is revocable at its pleasure. A decision of one of the Australian courts that the administration of Victoria could not of its own motion, without a statute, direct aliens to be

[1] Chae Chang Ping *vs.* The Collector of the Port of San Francisco.

kept out,[1] seems to turn on a question of administrative law, and cannot mean that neither the colony nor the British Parliament would possess the right to keep aliens out of the colony. It is perfectly natural that in the case of the Chinese the British government should desire to proceed by way of diplomatic negotiation so as not to hurt the feelings of a friendly nation, or complicate its foreign relations, and with that end it may refuse to give the assent of the crown to colonial legislation. But if diplomatic negotiations fail, there is no doubt that the crown will be obliged to yield to the desires of the colonies.

Popular sentiment in the United States, while condemning the way the Chinese have been treated, has for the most part acquiesced in their exclusion. The old ground of inalienable right to migrate has been abandoned, and we are content that a race which seems so difficult of amalgamation with our own should be kept at a distance. Humanitarian dreams of the equality of all men of all races and degrees of civilization have retired into the background as the difficulty of applying such principles to the practical problems of social life has been experienced. The new rule as to the exact duty which a nation owes to the citizens of other nations who desire to take up their residence with it has not yet been clearly formulated. But experience will doubtless bring that also in due time.

[1] London Times, Oct. 17, 1888.

CHAPTER XII.

RESTRICTIONS ON IMMIGRATION.

IT has already been said that freedom of emigration is restricted by the obligation to discharge military duty, although otherwise the subject of almost any civilized state has the right to expatriate himself. In like manner the right of immigration is not perfect, but is subject to certain restrictions applying partly to the admission of the stranger and partly to his continued residence in the state. All of these restrictions rest on the broad ground of the sovereignty of the nation over its own territory, which cannot possibly be limited by the right of foreigners to stay there against the desire of the state. To admit any other principle would be to limit the sovereignty of the state by the sovereignty of some other state. Arrangements may be made by treaty, but these are always revocable at the pleasure of either government, at the risk, of course, of giving a *casus belli* to the other party.

This absolute right to expel aliens or to refuse them admission has often been exercised; hitherto, indeed, with no idea of restricting the movement of migration, but solely from political and police considerations. It is only within the last ten years that there has been displayed a disposition to restrict immigration on account of the general economic or social interests of the country.

The right to expel aliens has always been maintained by the governments of Europe as a means of protecting themselves against political conspirators. In France, for instance, the law of December 3, 1849, permits the expulsion of foreigners by simple ministerial decree, but the meaning of this law is explained as follows:

> "It has been only too clearly shown that the plots which threaten not only the government, but the entire order of society, are framed by a vast organization of agitators, who, having given up the idea of a fatherland, go wherever there is an opportunity for disturbance, and who, as soon as their criminal enterprises have failed, recruit their ranks on the territory of the neighboring country. Society will not regain perfect security until all European nations refuse to extend hospitality to the secret meetings of these wandering agitators, and it lies with the government to distinguish them from true defenders of the liberty and the nationality of the peoples, with whom they are too often confounded." [1]

As political agitation has been succeeded by socialistic agitation, which is eminently cosmopolitan, the

---

[1] Report of M. de Montigny, quoted in Laws of Foreign Countries respecting the Admission and Continued Residence of Destitute Aliens, p. 27. House of Commons Paper, 1887.

wish has often been entertained by governments to come to some mutual understanding by which the right of asylum of these enemies of the existing order should be restricted. When the International Association of Workingmen began to spread, the Spanish administration addressed a circular note to the governments of Europe proposing common measures against the organization, and in this was warmly supported by Prince Bismarck; but the proposal failed on account of the refusal of Great Britain. A few years ago, however, Great Britain expelled Most on account of his socialistic writings, and there is a growing desire on the part of the English newspapers to reach the Irish agitators who, from the friendly shelter of this country, conduct the dynamite campaign against the British government. Very recently several nations have tried to browbeat Switzerland into expelling from her soil socialistic agitators who had taken refuge there. And one of the measures suggested after the anarchistic outbreaks in Chicago was that the President of the United States should expel from the country all the aliens engaged in the agitation. All these cases have only a political interest.

Immigration or the right to take up a permanent residence is often restricted by police measures intended to secure the community against the domiciliation of undesirable persons. In former times this police supervision (including the necessity of having a passport in order to cross the frontier) was very severe, but in modern times it is much relaxed. It generally consists in the requirement that a stranger who desires to take up a permanent residence in the country shall report himself to the police authorities, producing evidence as to his nationality, his good character, and in some cases that he has the means of supporting himself. The last provision is a tradition of the old administration of the poor law, which universally allowed a commune to refuse admission to a person who was liable to come on the poor relief. These police regulations are now generally administered with intelligence and great leniency, so that the ordinary stranger has no trouble in securing the right to reside in any country he likes. Thus in Italy the "Minister of the Interior urges the greatest toleration towards foreigners whose papers are not perfectly regular since the government has decided (in 1860) no longer to demand travellers' passports. The police are to be satisfied with the production of any kind of document proving the identity of the individual. No special permission is required by an alien for establishing his domicile in the Kingdom of Italy."[1]

In exceptional cases these police measures are made more severe. Such has been the case in Ger-

---

[1] Laws of Foreign Countries, etc., p. 35.

many, where large cities have been placed in the state of petty siege (*kleiner Belagerungszustand*), and extraordinary powers have been conferred on the police by the Anti-Socialistic laws. Such also seems to be the case on the Polish frontier, where the German government has expelled the Slavic population and is endeavoring to colonize the country with Germans. Such are the extraordinary measures of the Russian government in the expulsion of Jews and the refusal to receive them again. The latest legislative movement in this direction is the new French decree (October 2, 1888) for the registration of foreigners. That law requires that:

"Every foreigner proposing to reside in France must within a fortnight of his arrival make a declaration to the authorities: Of nationality; of place and date of birth; of last place of residence; of profession or means of livelihood; of name, age and nationality of wife and children (minors) when accompanied by them. Documents have to be produced in support of this declaration. In each case of change of residence a fresh declaration has to be made. Infractions of these rules will be punishable with police penalties, independently of the right of expulsion vested in the Minister of the Interior."[1]

The importance of these provisions lies in the fact that they are not merely police measures such as those noted above, but have originated in dissatisfaction on account of the number of foreigners in

[1] Translation of the regulation printed in The Board of Trade Journal, Nov., 1888.

France. That number has trebled since 1851, and now constitutes three per cent of the total population. These foreigners, especially the Italians, work for less wages than the French workmen, and are free from the military service which is such a burden. The above measure will probably be followed by some special taxation or restriction on the employment of foreigners in French factories. If so, it marks a distinct departure in the legislation of Europe in regard to immigration and the treatment of aliens.[1]

[1] The following extract from The Economist, July 2, 1887, shows the extent of the feeling in France against foreigners: "Nearly two years back, in November, 1885, a number of bills were presented to the French Chamber of Deputies, with the object of protecting French labor and trade from foreign competition. One proposed, that in contracts for public works for the state, the departments, or the communes, the contractors should be bound to employ French workmen only; another, that only French materials should be used; a third, that all stores for the public services, oats for the army, coal for the navy, etc., should be French exclusively, unless they were articles not produced in France; a fourth demanded that, except in case of absolute necessity, no foreigners should be admitted as purveyors to the state; a fifth proposed a tax on foreign workmen and *employés*, etc. These bills were all referred to one committee, but until the last few days nothing more had been heard of them. Recent events in Alsace-Lorraine have, perhaps, led to their being taken up afresh, for the committee has set seriously to work to draw up a bill embodying all those desiderata, and the Minister of Foreign Affairs had, this week, an interview with the committee to give his views as to how far such measures would be compatible with the existing treaties of commerce. The question of the liability of foreigners to military service was also raised in the discussion on the Army Bill, which is now before the French Chamber. M. Flourens was of opinion that the treaties of

There is one other class of cases where it has been a problem what to do with aliens : that is, when they are actual beggars and vagabonds. The laws of all states allow these persons to be treated just as the citizens of the same class are treated, that is, subjected to police punishment, imprisonment, hard labor, etc., and in some cases prescribe that they shall be expelled or sent back to their native country. Belgium once pursued the policy of conducting to the nearest frontier destitute aliens who had been arrested by the police. She was soon confronted with the difficulty that the different countries on her frontier refused to receive any but their own subjects. By a convention with Luxemburg that frontier

commerce did not permit such restrictions, but he suggested means by which the stipulations of the treaties might be evaded. With regard to the employment of foreign workmen and the use of foreign material, he said that any legislative exclusion would be contrary to the text of the treaties, but the state and the communes could introduce whatever conditions they pleased in the contracts they made; meaning that clauses might be introduced imposing French material and French workmen. That idea had, however, been already acted on before it was suggested by the Minister of Foreign Affairs. The exhibition committee held a meeting last week to invite tenders for works, and decided that no foreign firms or companies, even those established in France and employing French workmen only, should be admitted. M. Flourens also gave as his opinion that although foreign workmen could not be taxed, they might be made to pay for exemption from military service if the Army Bill contained a clause requiring payment from French citizens exempt from military service. In that case the tax would be extended to all persons not liable to serve in the army, including foreigners."

Restrictions on Immigration. 273

was closed to all except natives, Italian subjects and Swiss citizens. By a convention with Germany none except those of German nationality were to be sent to her. It was the custom of the Dutch gendarmerie to reconduct to the Belgian frontier all French, Italian and Spanish subjects who had been expelled by Belgium. The latter country was obliged to modify the ordinance so that the indigent alien should be sent to the country to which he belonged. The difficulty has sometimes been met by treaty agreement, by which two countries agree to admit the subjects of the other to the right of poor-relief. Such a convention, for instance, is in force between Germany and Austria-Hungary, by which subjects of the German Empire in Austria-Hungary, and subjects of Austria-Hungary in the German Empire will be admitted to poor law relief on the same conditions and under the same legal provisions as the native subjects of the country in which application for relief is made.[1]

The most advanced legislation in regard to immigration is that of the United States. As we have already seen, this country has always protested against the sending of paupers and criminals to her shores by the countries of Europe as a violation of international comity. The state of New York through her State Board of Charities has sent pauper aliens back to the country of birth, but at

---

[1] Laws of Foreign Countries, etc., p. 30.

her own expense. Still further, by her legislation New York made the steamship companies responsible for immigrants that were unable to support themselves. This legislation having been declared unconstitutional so far as the imposition of a tax was concerned, it was superseded by the act of Congress of 1882. This act, after providing for a head tax of fifty cents on every immigrant by sea and for the inspection of vessels by commissioners empowered thereto by the Secretary of the Treasury, goes on to say:

"And if on such examination there shall be found among such passengers any convict, lunatic, idiot, or any person unable to take care of himself or herself without becoming a public charge, they shall report the same in writing to the collector of the port, and such person shall not be permitted to land."

Section 4 of this act provides:

"That all foreign convicts, except those convicted of political offences, upon arrival, shall be sent back to the nations to which they belong and from whence they came. . . . The expense of such return of the aforesaid persons not permitted to land shall be borne by the owners of the vessels in which they came."

It has been decided, under this act, that landing persons at Castle Garden for the purpose of inspection is not landing within the meaning of the law, but that after they have left Castle Garden they are beyond the power of the commissioners and can no longer be returned. It is for the convenience of all persons concerned that the inspection should take place in Castle Garden rather than on board ship. Still further, it has been decided that whether a person is unable to take care of himself or herself, must be determined in each case, and the fact that a person has been assisted to emigrate is not sufficient evidence on which to reject him. The final decision as to whether persons shall be permitted to land lies with the collector of the port, and not with the commissioners of emigration. The law has been declared constitutional by the Supreme Court, as a regulation of commerce.[1]

The number of immigrants sent back under this act from the port of New York was in 1883, 1294; in 1884, 1363; in 1885, 1322; in 1886, 997; in 1887, 443; in 1888, 502. During the last named year 707 immigrants were reported by the commissioners to the collector of the port as being of the prohibited classes, but of this number only 502 were returned by the collector. In addition, 569 persons unable to maintain themselves were returned to Europe, their passage having been paid wholly or in part by the commissioners of emigration.[2]

This division of power between the commissioners and the collector seems to be a bad thing and will probably have to be remedied by placing the execu-

---
[1] Eyde *vs.* Robertson. Decided Dec. 8, 1884.
[2] Reports of Commissioners of Emigration.

tion of the whole law in the hands of paid officials of the United States. The inspection, also, is hurried and inefficient as is necessarily the case when thousands are landed in a single day and inspected by a small number of officers.

The legislation of the United States has gone still further in restricting immigration, by the passage of the law prohibiting the importation of laborers under contract. The original act of 1885 provided in brief:

That it shall be unlawful for any person, company, partnership, or corporation to prepay the transportation or in any way assist or encourage the importation or migration of any alien or aliens, into the United States under contract or agreement to perform labor or service of any kind in the United States. All such contracts are made void; a penalty of $1000 is imposed on persons violating the law, and of $500 on ship captains knowingly bringing contract laborers. Exceptions are made in favor of professional actors, artists, lecturers, or singers, and persons engaged strictly as domestic servants, and skilled laborers in industries not yet established in the United States. By an amendatory act of 1887 vessels are to be inspected in the same way as by the act of 1882, and if any contract laborers are found they are not to be permitted to land, but must be sent back at the expense of the owners of the vessels in which they came. By further amendments in 1888 provision is made for the payment to informers of not to exceed fifty per cent of the penalties recovered; and also that if an immigrant lands contrary to the provisions of the act he can still be sent back within one year of his landing.[1]

The provisions of this act do not seem to be very well enforced, owing to the difficulty of procuring evidence as to the actual contract or agreement.

Such, together with the Chinese exclusion bill mentioned in the previous chapter, is the legislation of the United States up to the present time. The committee of Congress commonly known as the Ford Immigration Committee recommended a much more severe enactment, but it never became law. It proceeded on the assumption of the absolute right of the United States to exclude from its territory any alien for any reason whatsoever. There is no doubt that such portion of the preceding legislation as is intended to prevent the coming of defectives and delinquents will remain a part of our law. Whether we shall go further and put absolute restrictions on immigration is a question not yet decided by legislation.

The whole argument of this book has been to show that it is desirable to correct certain evils which

[1] All these acts are printed in Report of Emigration Commissioners of New York, 1889.

flow from perfect freedom of immigration. When we ask what is the best method of doing this, the question is difficult to answer. Of the various legislative methods, noted above, none has as yet proven entirely satisfactory. In seeking a remedy for the present abuses there is constant danger that we may be simply groping back to mediæval restrictions and vexations which are incompatible with the conditions of modern life. There is danger also that a spirit of chauvinism, or of petty trade jealousy, or of demagogy may take possession of the movement, and exploit it for its own contemptible purposes. The control of immigration must be free from the base cry of "America for the Americans," and from any narrow spirit of trade-unionism, or of a selfish desire to monopolize the labor market. It must find its justification in the needs of the community, and in the necessity of selecting those elements which will contribute to the harmonious development of our civilization. The end to be desired is perfectly plain. It is, that immigration shall be controlled in such a way that elements incompatible with our civilization shall be excluded; that the defective and delinquent classes, who are only a burden and a danger to us, shall also be excluded; and that the immigration shall not be on such a scale as to threaten the integrity of our political institutions or to cause economic disturbances. The general method is to establish some process of selection by which the immigration of undesirable persons shall be discouraged.

From this point of view it is apparent that absolute prohibition of immigration is neither necessary nor desirable. The only exception is perhaps in the case of men of an alien civilization like the Chinese, who do not seem disposed to relinquish their own habits and customs for those of their adopted land. The homogeneity of our civilization seems to demand that they shall be excluded. The only question here is when the danger point is reached. But the demands of modern life would make the absolute prohibition of immigration from Europe burdensome and oppressive. It would be impossible, for instance, to prevent the friends and relatives of those already here from joining them. Great transportation interests are involved which it would be unfair to destroy suddenly and without notice. Absolute prohibitions directed against immigrants of any particular nationality are invidious, and would be apt to provoke retaliation. Our measures should be such as are practicable to enforce, and such as shall have the effect of gradually discouraging immigration until it shall be of good quality and of reasonable dimensions. Our political institutions and economic prosperity must take care of the rest.

The first and most obvious of all these measures

is the rigid enforcement of the present laws against the landing of paupers, criminals and persons unable to support themselves. That these laws are not enforced is a scandal to the community. There is no question as to the entire undesirability of such immigration both for us and for the persons themselves. It is difficult to make the inspection successful when the immigrants land by the thousand at Castle Garden, but additional inspectors could make it more successful than it is now. If the whole matter were put into the hands of United States officials, it might insure more thoroughness and some uniformity of procedure at the different ports. Still further, the steamship companies should be held rigidly responsible for bringing over persons who are prohibited by law from landing. Thereby part of the work of inspection would be transferred to them, and they would exercise some discrimination as to the kind of people to whom they sell tickets. Assisted emigration, whether the assistance comes from foreign governments or local authorities or charitable societies should be protested against, and made a subject of diplomatic negotiation.

The law against the importation of laborers under contract should also be enforced as far as it is possible. It will not be possible to detect every case where a man comes under promise of employment; nor are these isolated cases of any particular consequence. The real evil of contract labor is that it offers an opportunity for the establishment of a system of induced immigration. Irresponsible private parties gather together ignorant laborers, and under promise of plentiful work on this side of the water, persuade them to come here, abandoning them as soon as they have made what they can out of them. To stop such a business as this is not interfering with any sound freedom of contract or of migration, while it stops the growth of what in the long run is pretty apt to become a sort of coolie traffic.

Among the measures recently proposed for the restriction of immigration, the most feasible, in my opinion, is the requirement of a consular certificate from emigrants. The following plan has the approval of Mr. Eugene Schuyler.[1] Every person who desires to emigrate to the United States shall be required to give notice to the nearest United States consular office, and the consul shall thereupon cause an inquiry to be instituted as to the person's character and past history and also his economic condition, whether he is likely to become a burden on our poor rates, etc.; and if his inquiries are satisfactory he shall issue consular certificates in triplicate, one copy to be

[1] Political Science Quarterly, vol. iv, p. 490. This particular plan is credited to Mr. George L. Catlin, United States consul at Zurich, but similar proposals came from several other consuls in their reports on emigration.

retained in his office, a second to be forwarded to the collector of the port or emigration commissioner, and the third to be given to the emigrant. No emigrant shall be permitted to land without the presentation of such a certificate. Two objections have been made to this scheme. One is that it would involve our consular offices in a great amount of clerical labor and expense. This might be met by charging a fee for the certificate, which might act as a wholesome deterrent on the emigration of poor or thoughtless persons. The second objection is that our consular officers would be dependent largely on the police authorities for their information, and these might seize the opportunity to hinder the emigration of desirable citizens and favor that of undesirable ones. It is not probable that the police records, which are kept with great minuteness in Europe, would be manipulated for such a purpose. There would be enough persons interested, the emigrants themselves, their friends this side of the water, the emigration agents, the United States officer, — to secure justice in most cases. To carry out such a system we must put ourselves into friendly communication with the governments of Europe, and co-operate with the system they are establishing to prevent the evils of emigration. We must recognize that they also are interested in the question, and assist them in their efforts to prevent the evasion of services due the state. With mutual good-will it would seem possible to control the movement so that it would be an injury to neither the old country nor the new. So far as we are concerned, it would be simply transferring the work of inspection from this side of the water, where it can never be efficiently performed, to the other side where it ought to be done. If it involves us in additional expense and trouble, we must recognize the fact that it is another case of relations becoming so important that they cannot be allowed to take care of themselves, but must be regulated. The problem is not easy of solution. Unrestricted immigration involves us in numerous difficulties. On the other hand, we do not wish to compromise the principle of freedom any further than we can help. The only alternative is to subject the movement to such control that the dangers shall be removed.

CHAPTER XIII.

THE QUESTION OF PRINCIPLE.

It has been shown in the preceding chapters that the nations of the world are actively asserting their right to regulate the admission or continued residence of aliens in their territory. The strict legal right of each nation to do this is not seriously disputed. It is well, however, to carry the investigation one step further and inquire how the right to restrict migration is looked upon from the standpoint of the comity of nations and of a theoretical political science which is not governed by considerations of mere temporary expediency.

And first, in regard to the right of migration as a question of theoretical international law: How are we to interpret the practice and the declarations of nations? The various facts already displayed in the history of emigration and immigration and the legislation at present in force will enable us to deduce the following result.

Freedom of migration is no natural, inherent right of the individual. It is merely an historical right of very recent origin, never universally recognized, and at the present moment undergoing restriction rather than expansion. Human history has already gone through two stages on this question and is standing on the threshold of a third. These three stages are, the mediæval, the French Revolutionary, and the modern socialistic.

All mediæval life denied by its very constitution any right of the individual to migrate or to choose his own domicile. Social relations regulated by *status* could not permit individuals to withdraw at their own will, nor find a place for strangers not members of the local community. This is abundantly illustrated in any study of the position of strangers during the whole mediæval period. The English merchant was often prohibited "going beyond seas." The foreign merchant in England was obliged to seek the special protection of the king. Aliens occupied a suspicious position and were liable to be plundered or imprisoned in return for wrongs done the citizens of the country abroad. In Germany there existed the so-called *Wildfangsrecht*, by which a stranger could be reduced to the position of a serf. It was the rule that the strange air made the man unfree, and unless he belonged of *status* to the class of the privileged, he sank into that of the dependant. Police considerations required that a man should not entertain a stranger unless he were willing to be responsible for him. In other cases, a man could not withdraw from the community except by paying a fine which indemnified it for the loss; and often he could not settle in another community without paying a fine for the privilege of settling. All these restrictions are characteristic of the petty relations of mediæval life.

Even after the city and provincial relations of early mediæval times began to broaden out into the national life of the seventeenth and eighteenth centuries, the stranger was still looked upon with dislike. In commerce he was a rival, as witness the navigation acts of Cromwell and Charles II. Nations were often engaged in war, and monarchs looked upon the emigration of their subjects as decreasing their military strength. In manufactures it was feared that artisans might carry the secrets of trade to other countries. The growth of the system of legal poor relief made each community examine every accession to the population with jealous eye lest it should add to the burden. The English "act of settlement" did not hesitate to prohibit migration from parish to parish, and down to very recent years it was the undoubted right of every city in Germany to refuse settlement to a stranger unless he could prove that he had property or the means of earning his livelihood. In none of these cases was there supposed to be any right of the individual. It was a question for the community, whether it was willing to receive him or not.

The second stage was that which received the impress of the French Revolution, and which may be termed the period of individualism. Two factors worked together to destroy the restrictions of the old régime. One was the expansion of industry and commerce, which burst the narrow bonds of petty city and provincial life and strove to become national and international; the other was the revolutionary philosophy with its doctrine of individual liberty and equality. The introduction of machinery and manufacturing on a large scale, which resulted in the so-called factory system of modern times, destroyed the restrictions which bound a man to a certain trade and locality. The mediæval guilds with their numberless regulations and privileges gave way before the demand for large numbers of unskilled laborers to work at the machine. The apprenticeship of seven years, which had been required before a man could engage in an industry, was no longer necessary, and fell away. Women and children were employed in increasing numbers, and the abundant supply of labor thus obtained rendered nugatory the old regulations of wages and hours of labor. The factory drew laborers from other localities, and thus destroyed the restrictions on free migration which were connected with poor relief and the petty financial interests of narrow communal life.

So in a precisely similar way, the expansion of

commerce removed internal custom duties, river tolls and prohibitions and hindrances of all sorts; and even in international trade led to greater reciprocity or to partial or entire free trade. When commerce became international, the foreign merchant was allowed the privilege of coming and going, of residence, of protection of property and finally practically all the rights and privileges which the citizen enjoyed, except political rights. Freedom of travel and domicile were thus introduced, the passport system became for the most part a formality, and the old discriminations against aliens were abandoned. The natural corollary of the modern system of industry and commerce is freedom of occupation, of travel and of domicile; just as the natural consequence of the mediæval relations of *status* was the immobility of the individual.

The "natural rights" doctrine of the French Revolution has given a philosophic basis to this system of freedom of migration. The revolutionary declarations destroyed all that remained of the feudal relations of personal dependence. The spirit of liberty and equality released the serf from the soil, and finally abolished chattel slavery in its last remaining form. It gave its sanction to the abolition of all restrictions on trade and commerce, and even went so far in some cases as to enshrine freedom of trade as one of the inalienable rights of the individual. It reversed the doctrine of the Middle Ages, and declared that freedom was the natural *status* of a man, and that the free air made the stranger free without regard to his previous condition. It deduced from this the doctrine that a man has the right to go where he pleases, and to choose his own domicile. It has finally developed into a sort of cosmopolitan humanitarianism, which views the men of all nations and of all civilizations as of equal worth, and demands that we raise ourselves above the narrow egoism of nationality, and consider the interests of all humanity. In this view there are no national boundaries; the individual is a citizen of the world; the black man is the equal of the white; the Asiatic of the European; and perfect freedom of migration is one factor in bringing about the realization of the brotherhood of man.

No one can fail to recognize the enormous benefits which have accrued to the world through this doctrine of the brotherhood of man and the right of men of all nations to be treated like men. It lies at the bottom of much that makes our civilization what it is. It is under the influence of this feeling that we have treated the question of emigration and immigration during the greater part of this century. It has taught us in this country to welcome the immigrant of whatever nationality or condition of life he may be. We have tacitly pinned our faith to the doctrine of the perfectibility of man, at least under the influence of free institutions. The climax of this movement was reached when we negotiated the treaties by which the nations of Europe acknowledged the right of expatriation, and we declared it to be a natural and inalienable right of the individual. It is under the influence of this doctrine that restrictions on emigration and immigration seem such doubtful measures. They seem to break with a fundamental principle of modern civilization, and to lead us back to that period when civil and political liberty were at the mercy of government. Before entering, therefore, upon the consideration of the third period, that of restriction of migration, on the threshold of which recent legislation seems to plant us, it will be well to consider this doctrine of freedom in all its different phases.

In the first place, we must disabuse ourselves of the notion that freedom of migration rests upon any right of the individual. It is simply a privilege granted by the state, the product of circumstances, the result of expediency. The state, therefore, that conferred the liberty may also withdraw it. The state that feels a loss of strength by emigration may forbid its inhabitants leaving the country. The state that suffers injury from immigration may put restrictions on persons coming to its shores, — may keep them out altogether if it so choose. The individual has no rights at all in the premises. Although he may possibly elude the watchfulness of the government that is trying to detain him, he cannot compel another state to receive him. Whatever may be his position towards his home government, as to the foreign state he has absolutely no rights. Any privileges that he may enjoy rest on diplomatic agreement, or on the legislation of the receiving state, not on any virtue residing in him. The individual has no right to force himself into a territory where he is not wanted.

But although freedom of immigration rests on no right of the individual, yet it is sometimes held that there is a cosmopolitan duty to admit other persons to the soil if they desire to come. A nation, it is said, has a right to the soil only on condition of making the best use of it, and if it have more land than it really need, it is in duty bound to share it with others. It is on this basis that the colonization of America by the nations of Europe is theoretically justified. The Indians were the original occupiers, and as such they owned the country. But the white men were more highly civilized, and could make better use of the land. What once barely kept a few thousand savages from starvation, now sustains millions of men in an advanced stage of culture. So it is said that the present inhabitants of the United States have no right to appropriate a country fitted to support several times their number. Especially is this true in sight of the millions of Europe who could find here comfort which they can never hope to attain at home. We have no right to keep these struggling millions out from our fertile fields and broad prairies.

This principle seems to me a perfectly sound one, but it is difficult to apply it so as to justify perfect freedom of migration. It *is* the right of the higher civilization to make the lower give way before it. It was this right that the nations of Europe felt was their justification in taking possession of this new country. It would be the same right that would justify Germany and Belgium and Italy in founding colonies in Africa. The higher civilization has a moral right to triumph over the lower, for it is in this way that the world progresses. The duty of every nation to humanity is to see to it that the higher does triumph over the lower. But it performs this duty best by preserving its own civilization against the disintegrating forces of barbarism. And when men demand admission who seem to be of a lower rather than of a higher stage of culture, their right to be admitted does not seem so plain. They may degrade the higher civilization without materially raising their own. A conquest by barbarians does not raise even the average civilization of the world. It destroys without replacing. And even if it did in some slight degree raise the average of human life, it would not be a gain. One nation on a high plane of civilization is better than half the world in a state of semi-civilization. There is this danger in indiscriminate immigration; it may be composed of elements which tend to pull down rather than build up. The admission of such elements does not help humanity at large, while it may destroy the standard of culture of the nationality receiving them.

There is, finally, one argument which is appealed to whenever it is proposed to restrict immigration to America. It is a wide-spread sentimental feeling that America has always been the home of the poor, the refuge of the oppressed of all nations. It is felt that we have always held our doors open, and that it is a betrayal of duty to shut them the moment we feel inconvenienced by our missionary work. I conceive that there is a double misunderstanding here. In the first place, our fathers, when they spoke of this country as the "asylum of the oppressed," meant that here should be a refuge from religious and political oppression. They meant that this should be the land of freedom, that all who came here should have liberty of conscience, liberty of opinion, of speech, etc. This country has on the whole remained faithful to this proclamation. Religious and political refugees of all nations have flocked hither, and we have not only extended protection to the new-comers, but have admitted them to a full share in the government itself. Our fathers did not mean that we were to be an asylum for the paupers, the convicts and the cripples of all nations. They did not mean asylum in the modern, limited signification of the word. It is true that many of the early immigrants were indentured as servants and obliged to work out their passage money after they came; but we do not find but that the colonists took the true view of these comers. They received them on account of the dearth of labor, but they would gladly have had better.

In the second place, there is liability to grave error in reasoning from the past experience of a country to infallible rules for its guidance in the future. A new country passes through successive stages where its needs and its demands are entirely different. At its first settlement the need is for labor, and any kind of labor is acceptable. As the nation advances in the agricultural stage, the need still is for labor. So long as unoccupied territory remains, so long as roads are to be built, canals dug, the country opened up, the need still is for labor. It is in this stage that free immigration is of benefit both to the country and to the immigrant. Even if the immigration is not of the highest type, the rough, hard life has a purifying effect, or at least prevents much damage being done. The immigrant meets with elements as rough as himself, and one controls the other. But as a nation progresses it loses this capacity of absorbing the lower elements of other civilizations. It no longer possesses the purifying power. It has all it can attend to with its own unfortunates. The struggle for existence increases in severity, and it can no longer offer to the immigrant the advantages it once did. He finds in the new country very much the same conditions as in the old, and labors under many disadvantages, such as ignorance of the language, customs and habits of life. It is no kindness to the immigrant to allow him to come under mistaken notions of the conditions of life here. No social science teaches that we should leave great masses of men to the guidance of blind impulse or chance. Neither is it just to our own citizens to introduce a mass of men, who may increase the competition in the labor market and lower the standard of living, without any regard to the ultimate consequences of thus following a principle which at one time may have been right, but which now needs modification. No general principle inherited from "the fathers" is sufficient to guide us in the treatment of such a problem as indiscriminate immigration with all the consequences therein involved.

We come now to the third period, upon which the state is just entering, viz., the control of the right of migration by positive law or by international agreement. An inherent right of migration is seen to be untenable in theory, and unrestricted emigration and immigration have been proven bad in practice. The only course that remains is to acknowledge the right of a state to regulate the emigration of its own citizens and the immigration of strangers, or for states to reach a diplomatic agreement for the purpose. It is true that no state has ever renounced the right to regulate both emigration and immigration, and it would be impossible for a state so to do without abandoning its own sovereignty; but there is now a disposition to exercise these rights for the purpose of escaping the evils of indiscriminate migration. This has been abundantly illustrated in the legislation which was noticed in the preceding chapters. The states whence emigration proceeds are determined to see to it that the business shall be conducted in such a way that it shall neither injure the state nor deceive the intending emigrant. The interests of the community over-ride those of persons engaged in the business of transportation, and can subordinate even the interests of the emigrants if they come in conflict with those of the state. There is no doubt that the states of Europe are perfectly right in this action. There is still less doubt that their disposition is to restrict emigration as much as possible, and with the present sentiment in this country and the British colonies there is no likelihood that any protest will be heard.

The Question of Principle. 297

The recent legislation of the United States points no less clearly to the limitation of immigration. Such action may proceed either against certain specified classes on the ground that they will become a burden to the community, or against a whole race on the ground that their civilization is not desirable. The extension of this legislation is only a question of the pressure exerted by immigration. If it remains where it is or decreases, we shall probably remain satisfied with our present measures. If it should increase or deteriorate in character, more drastic measures will be proposed. Our example in regard to the Chinese has already been followed by the Australians and British Columbians; and England and France show a disposition to legislate against the incoming of poor foreign workmen. It is not probable that any country will protest against the principle that each nation has the right to regulate the matter for itself, although the countries of Europe may demand reciprocity of treatment among themselves.

The principles of international law upon which the modern practice is to be based may be seen emerging in several directions. The right to restrict emigration will be founded on a revival of the doctrine of permanent allegiance to the state, modified by international agreement. That doctrine, once so powerful, has been undermined by the spirit of individualism, and by the practical necessities of new countries where permanent settlers could not be held in subordination to governments which they had expressly renounced. An attempt has been made to formulate this practical necessity into an absolute right of the individual to change his allegiance whenever he pleases, but this has led to numerous difficulties. One is that it opens the way for evasion of those duties which every citizen owes to the state, such as in Europe the universal military duty, and to this no state can as a matter of principle consent, however many exceptions and modifications it may allow in practice. Another is that the new allegiance may be acquired and used simply for the purpose of escaping the burdens of the old, and no state can afford to stake its influence or existence on the protection of citizens whose citizenship is merely nominal and for the purpose of commercial gain. The experience of the United States with its Irish-American and German-American citizens has proven this. Finally, this right to change one's allegiance every time one finds it profitable so to do, has complicated the whole system of international obligation, and has even led to men being without a country.

The modern tendency is seen in the following extract from a recent writer on international law, which, although the writer is an Englishman and prejudiced perhaps in favor of the dictum "once an

Englishman always an Englishman," is a fair presentation of the question. After citing the recent cases where the question of expatriation has come up, the author goes on to say:

"It may be taken that the practice of the foregoing states gives a fair impression of practice as a whole; and it may be assumed that when a state makes the recognition of a change of nationality by a subject dependent on his fulfilment of certain conditions determined by itself, or when it concedes a right of expatriation by express law, it in effect affirms a doctrine of allegiance indissoluble except by consent of the state. Such being the case the doctrine in question, disguised though it may be, is still the groundwork of a vastly preponderant custom. It may be hoped, both for reasons of theory and convenience, that it will continue to be so. An absolute right of expatriation involves the anarchical principle that an individual, as such, has other rights as against his state in things connected with the state society than the right not to be dealt with arbitrarily, or dissimilarly from others circumstanced like himself, which is implied in the conception of a duly ordered political community; it supposes that the individual will is not necessarily subordinated to the common will in matters of general concernment. As a question of convenience, the objections to admitting a right of expatriation are fully as strong. The right, if it exists, is absolute; it can therefore be curtailed only with the consent of each individual. But if the doctrine of permanent allegiance be admitted, there is nothing to prevent the state from tempering its application to any extent that may be deemed proper. Action upon it in its crude form is obviously incompatible with the needs of modern life; but it is consistent with any terms of international agreement which the respective interests of contracting parties may demand, and if recognized in principle and taken as an interim rule where special agreements have not been made, it would do away with practical inconveniences which frequently occur, and which as between certain countries might in some cases give rise to international dangers. It would be a distinct gain if it were universally acknowledged that it is the right of every state to lay down under what conditions its subjects may escape from their nationality of origin, and that the acquisition of a foreign nationality must not be considered good by the state granting it as against the country of origin unless the conditions have been satisfied." Hall, International Law, p. 214.

The right to restrict or prohibit immigration is based ultimately on the sovereignty of a state over its own territory. It can suffer no abatement of that sovereignty on the part of other states, and still less on the part of individuals, except by international agreement. That the consensus of civilized nations will allow a large measure of freedom of intercourse and of trade and even of settlement there is no doubt. The demands of modern life will secure that. And so far as the evils of indiscriminate immigration are concerned, the practical rule is already coming to be recognized that it is not a friendly act on the part of other nations to allow the emigration of persons whom the receiving state does not consider desirable additions to its population. In practice no state would defend the right to ship its convicts or paupers to another state, or disregard the protest of that other state. And out of this practical rule will there not finally be developed the general principle that each nation is bound to provide for its own unfortunates? They are a part of that society the whole of which constitutes the state. They are as much its citizens as their more fortunate neighbors. Out of the abundance of the civilization there must come provision for its weaknesses. We cannot retain only that which is good and cast that which is maimed into outer darkness.

And after all is it not a higher ideal, not only of international comity but also of humanity, that each nation should provide for its own failures rather than attempt to transfer the duty to some other nation? If there be no room for them let them be sent away with at least some provision for starting in the new country, so that they shall not be a total burden. Emigration has not proven a remedy either for over-population or for wide-spread poverty and distress. There remains the attempt to better the condition of the poor at home. Modern socialistic legislation in its effort to improve the sanitary surroundings of the laboring classes in home and factory, by its insurance against old age, accident and sickness, by its provision for education and culture, is slowly weaving a web about the workman which will bind him more closely to his native country. It is possible that this will provide for those whom no man desires, while leaving sufficient freedom to the stronger and more enterprising to work out their own destiny. Freedom of international intercourse and movement will thus be preserved, while the hardships and evils of the present unguided, ignorant and capricious migration will be prevented.

BIBLIOGRAPHY.[1]

ALTENBERG, A., Deutsche Auswanderungsgesetzgebung. Berlin, 1885.

ASCHROTT AND PRESTON-THOMAS, English Poor Law System, pp. 42, 200 and 225. London, 1888.

BECKER, KARL, Unsere Verluste durch Wanderung, Schmoller's Jahrbücher für Gesetzgebung, etc., XI. S. 765. Leipzig, 1887.

BEMIS, E. W., Restrictions on Immigration, The Andover Review, March, 1888.

BEMIS, E. W., The Distribution of our Immigrants, The Andover Review, June, 1888.

BOARD OF TRADE JOURNAL, June, 1888, November, 1888, March, 1889, April, 1889, and June, 1889. London, 1888 and 1889.

BODIO, LUIGI, Sulla Condizione dell' Emigrazione Italiana. Roma, 1888.

BONNEY, C. C., Naturalization Laws and their Enforcement, The New Englander, Vol. 13, p. 305, November, 1888.

BRABAZON, LORD, State-Directed Emigration, The Nineteenth Century, November, 1884.

BROMWELL, WM. J., History of Immigration into the United States. New York, 1856.

BULLETIN DE L'INSTITUT INTERNATIONAL DE STATISTIQUE.
    Tome I. 2ème livraison, p. 25.
    Tome II. 2ème livraison, pp. 37 and 95.
    Tome III. Premiere livraison, p. 136. Rome, 1887–1889.

---

[1] NOTE. — *Laws and Treaties are to be found in the Statutes at Large; debates in the Congressional Record; and numerous other magazine articles by reference to Poole's Index to Periodicals.*

CENSUS (TENTH) OF THE UNITED STATES, Vols. I., Population; II., Manufactures; III., Agriculture; XI. and XII., Mortality and Vital Statistics; XXI., Defective, Dependent and Delinquent Classes. Washington, 1883-1889.

CHICKERING, Immigration into the United States. Boston, 1848.

CHINESE IMMIGRATION, REPORT OF THE JOINT COMMITTEE OF THE SENATE AND HOUSE OF REPRESENTATIVES ON, 1876. Washington, 1877.

COLONIZATION. Report from the Select Committee of the House of Commons. London, 1889.

COMMISSIONERS OF EMIGRATION OF THE STATE OF NEW YORK, REPORTS OF THE, 1847-1860. New York, 1861.

Do. Reports, 1861-1889, annually.

CONNECTICUT BUREAU OF LABOR STATISTICS, REPORT FOR 1885.

CORRESPONDENCE RESPECTING THE ADMISSION INTO THE UNITED STATES OF DESTITUTE ALIENS AND STATE-AIDED IMMIGRANTS. London, 1887.

CORRESPONDENCE FROM COLONIAL GOVERNMENTS IN ANSWER TO MEMORANDUM BY PARLIAMENTARY COLONIZATION COMMITTEE OF MAY 1, 1888. Two Returns. London, 1889.

DANA, DR. C. L., Immigration and Nervous Diseases, in Papers of American Social Science Association, 1888.

DAWES, H. L., The Chinese Exclusion Bill, The Forum, January, 1889.

DEE, M. J., Chinese Immigration, The North American Review, Vol. 126, p. 506, 1878.

DEXTER, F. B., Estimates of Population in the American Colonies. Worcester, 1887.

ECONOMIST, THE. London, July 2, 1887, Oct. 6, 1888, Jan. 26, 1889, and Sept. 28, 1889.

EMIGRATION AND IMMIGRATION. Reports of Consular Officers of the United States. Washington, 1885-1886.

EMIGRATION AND IMMIGRATION (FOREIGNERS). Report of House of Commons Committee, 1888.
Do. 1889.
EMIGRANTS' INFORMATION OFFICE, REPORT OF. London, 1888 and 1889.
FARR, WILLIAM, Vital Statistics, p. 60. London, 1885.
FAWCETT, HENRY, Manual of Political Economy, pp. 145, 235 and 602. London, 1883.
FAWCETT, HENRY, The Economic Position of the British Laborer. London, 1865.
FOREIGN RELATIONS OF THE UNITED STATES, 1878, 1879, 1880 and 1881 (Switzerland); 1880 and 1888 (China).
GEFFCKEN, H., Bevölkerungspolitik, Auswanderung und Colonisation, in Schönberg's Handbuch der Politischeoekonomie, 2d ed. II. S. 943. Tübingen, 1886.
HERZOG, E., Was fliesst den Vereinigten Staaten durch die Einwanderung zu, etc., in Schmoller's Jahrbücher für Gesetzgebung, etc., IX. S. 31. Leipzig, 1885.
IMMIGRATION. Testimony and Reports of Committee of the House of Representatives to inquire into alleged violations of the Law, etc. Three Reports, Testimony, and Reports from Consuls. Washington, 1889.
IMMIGRATION. Report of the Standing Committee on Immigration, — with the Discussion thereon, — prepared and read before the National Conference of Charities and Correction, at Washington, D.C., June 9, 1885, by Dr. Chas. S. Hoyt.
INTERNATIONAL RECORD OF CHARITIES AND CORRECTION, September, 1887.
IOWA BUREAU OF LABOR STATISTICS, REPORT FOR 1885.
IRELAND, EMIGRATION STATISTICS OF, annually. Dublin.
JARVIS, DR. EDWARD, Immigration, Atlantic Monthly, Vol. XXIX. p. 468, April, 1872.
KANSAS BUREAU OF LABOR STATISTICS, REPORT FOR 1887.
KAPP, FRIEDRICH, Immigration and the Commissioners of Emigration of the State of New York. New York, 1870.

KAPP, FRIEDRICH, Ueber Auswanderung. Berlin, 1871.
KARRER, L., Das schweizerische Auswanderungswesen. Bern, 1886.
LAWS OF FOREIGN COUNTRIES RESPECTING THE ADMISSION AND CONTINUED RESIDENCE OF DESTITUTE ALIENS, House of Commons Paper, 1887.
LIÉGARD, ARMAND, Immigration into the United States, Translation in the Journal of the London Statistical Society, Vol. 47, p. 496, September, 1884.
LEROY-BEAULIEU, PAUL, De la colonisation chez les peuples modernes. 3d ed. Paris, 1886.
LOCAL GOVERNMENT BOARD, REPORT OF, 1886. London, 1886.
MASSACHUSETTS BUREAU OF LABOR STATISTICS, REPORT FOR 1887, The Unemployed. Boston, 1887.
MASSACHUSETTS, CENSUS OF, 1885, Vol. I. Parts 1 and 2. Boston, 1887 and 1888.
MEMORANDUM ON IMMIGRATION OF FOREIGNERS, Board of Trade Paper, April, 1887. London, 1887.
MICHIGAN, REPORT OF BUREAU OF LABOR STATISTICS, 1887.
MONKSWELL, LORD, State Colonization, The Fortnightly Review, March, 1888.
NEW JERSEY BUREAU OF LABOR STATISTICS, REPORT FOR 1884.
NEW YORK, STATE BOARD OF CHARITIES, REPORTS FOR 1887 AND 1888.
NEW YORK BUREAU OF LABOR STATISTICS, REPORT FOR 1885.
RAVENSTEIN, E. G., The Laws of Migration, Journal of the London Statistical Society, March, 1885, and June, 1889.
REPORTS ON THE STATUS OF ALIENS AND FOREIGN COMPANIES IN THE UNITED STATES. London, 1887.
ROBERT, Zur Auswanderungsfrage. Wien, 1879.
ROGERS, J. E. T., The Colonial Question, Cobden Club Essays, 2d series. London, 1872.
ROSCHER AND JANNASCH, Kolonien, Kolonialpolitik und Auswanderung. 3d ed. Leipzig, 1885.

ROSMINI, CESARE, Il nuovo Progetto di Legge sulla Emigrazione, Il Giornale degli Economisti, Vol. 3, p. 121, 1888.

ROUND, W. M. F., Immigration and Crime, The Forum, December, 1889.

RÜMELIN, Bevölkerungslehre, in Schönberg's Handbuch der Politischeoekonomie. 2 Ausg. II. S. 913. Leipzig, 1886.

SANDERSON, J. P., Republican Landmarks. Philadelphia, 1856.

SCALABRINI, G. B., L' Emigrazione italiana in America. Piacenza, 1887.

SCHUYLER, EUGENE, Italian Immigration, Political Science Quarterly, September, 1889.

SEWARD, G. F., Chinese Immigration. New York, 1881.

SEYBERT, Statistical Annals of the United States. Philadelphia, 1818.

SIMMONS, ALFRED, State Emigration, A Reply to Lord Derby. London, 1884.

STATISTICA DELL' EMIGRAZIONE ITALIANA PER GLI ANNI 1884 E 1885 CON NOTIZIE DI LEGISLAZIONE E STATISTICA COMPARATA. Roma, 1886.

STATISTICA DELL' EMIGRAZIONE ITALIANA, 1888. Roma, 1889.

STATISTICAL TABLES RELATING TO EMIGRATION AND IMMIGRATION FROM AND INTO THE UNITED KINGDOM. Board of Trade, annually. London.

STRONG, JUSTICE WM., Defective Naturalization Laws, North American Review, Vol. 138, p. 415, 1884.

SWEATING SYSTEM, REPORT OF COMMITTEE OF THE LORDS ON THE. Four Reports. London, 1888 and 1889.

SWEATING SYSTEM AT THE EAST END OF LONDON, REPORT ON, BY THE LABOUR CORRESPONDENT OF THE BOARD OF TRADE. London, 1887.

SWEATING SYSTEM IN LEEDS. Report of the Labour Correspondent of the Board of Trade. London, 1888.

TABLES SHOWING ARRIVALS OF ALIEN PASSENGERS AND IMMIGRANTS IN THE UNITED STATES FROM 1820 TO 1888, Treasury Department, March, 1889.

TIMES, THE LONDON, May 19, July 30, Sept. 5 and Sept. 18, 1888; Jan. 21, Jan. 22, May 27, July 19 and Oct. 17, 1889.

TUKE, J. H., State Aid to Emigrants, The Nineteenth Century, February, 1885.

WALKER, F. A., The Labor Problem of To-day, An Address before the Alumni Association of Lehigh University. New York, 1887.

WHARTON, International Law Digest, Vol. II. Washington, 1888.

WHITE, ARNOLD, Problems of Great Cities, Chapter IV., Emigration; V., Colonization. London, 1886.

WHITE, ARNOLD, The Invasion of Pauper Foreigners, The Nineteenth Century, March, 1888.

WHITNEY, J. A., The Chinese and the Chinese Question. New York, 1888.

WILLIAMS, S. W., Chinese Immigration, Journal of the American Social Science Association, 1879.

WISCONSIN BUREAU OF LABOR STATISTICS, REPORT FOR 1885–6.

WISCONSIN, FOREIGN IMMIGRATION IN, The Milwaukee Sentinel, March 10, 1889.

INDEX.

Age, of emigrants, 28; of immigrants, 51.
Age-classification, effect of, on statistics of insanity, crime and disease, 152.
Agriculture, foreign born persons engaged in, 94.
Alien paupers, removal of, by state of New York, 160; expulsion of, by Belgium, 272; treaty in regard to, between Germany and Austria-Hungary, 273.
Aliens, number of, in Massachusetts, 80; right to expel, 267.
Allegiance, doctrine of permanent, 297, 298.
Anti-Chinese agitation in California, 238.
Assimilation of foreign elements, 63, 65; influences towards, 73; difficulty of, in case of Chinese, 247.
Assisted emigration and immigration, chapter IX, 168-200; by Switzerland, 171; by British government, 173; by charitable societies, 176, 185; protest of U. S. against, 175; immigration by Canada, 193; by Australia, 194; Southern Association for, 195.
Asylum, doctrine that this country is an, for the oppressed, 251, 293.
Australia, assisted immigration to, 194; Chinese question in, 263.
Austria, emigration from, 19.
Austria-Hungary, paupers sent back to, 160; treaty between, and Germany in regard to paupers, 273. See also Hungary.

Bedridden among foreign born in Massachusetts, 156.
Belgium, emigration from, 19; emigrant's bureau at Buenos Ayres, 204; expels alien paupers, 272.
Bibliography, 303.
Births, excess of, over deaths compared with emigration, 23.
Blind among the foreign born, 155, 156.
Boston, persons of native and foreign parentage in, 71.
Bringing up children, cost of, 104.
British, see Great Britain.
British America (and British Americans), female immigrants from, 50; persons having fathers born in, 68; born in, 69; marriage of, 76 n.; engaged in productive occupations in U. S., 71, 96.
Brotherhood of man, doctrine of, 289.
Burlingame treaty with China, 229, 231.

Canada, assisted immigration to, 178, 185, 193. See also French Canadians.
Capitalized value of immigrant, 109.
Castle Garden, 221.
Charitable societies sending out paupers, 160, 176, 185.
Cheap labor, effect of, 143.
Chinese immigration, chapter XI, 227-265.
Cities, foreign born in, 71; unskilled labor in, 120.
Citizenship, a matter of choice, 201.
Civilization, characteristics of Amer-

309

ican, 4; progress of, renders demand for unskilled labor less, 119; what it consists of, 147; tenacity of Chinese in adhering to their own, 248; different stages in, 294.
Colonies, early, 12; effect of, on Europe, 13; separation from home country, 14; assist immigration, 169; opposition to assisted emigration, 184.
Colonists, task before, in the U. S., 53; distinction between, and immigrants, 35.
Colonization, committee of House of Commons, 180; of America, 291.
Commerce, regulation of, only by Congress, 241; expansion of, 287.
Commissioners of Emigration of New York, 220, 222, 225.
Committee of Congress on Chinese immigration, 242; report of, 250.
Competition, with American labor, chapter VII, 123-146; on a certain plane of living, 138; true office of, 141.
Connecticut, Italian immigrants in, 133.
Consular certificates, plan of, 281.
Consular jurisdiction, in China, 230.
Consular protection to emigrants, 204.
Conquest, early migration for purpose of, 12.
Contract labor, 129-131; legislation of U. S. against, 276; should be enforced, 279.
Control of immigration, methods of, 277-283.
Convicts, of foreign birth or parentage in Massachusetts, 157; exclusion of, by U. S., 274.
Criminals, among foreign born, 157.
Crippled, among foreign born, 156.

Deaf and dumb, among foreign born, 155; in Massachusetts, 156.
Deformed, among foreign born, in Massachusetts, 156.
Democratic institutions, smooth working of, 91.

Denmark, emigration from, 19; per 1000 inhabitants, 21; since 1820, 67; paupers returned to, 160.
Destination, avowed, of immigrants, 69.
Diseased, acute and chronic, among foreign born in Massachusetts, 156.
Distribution of foreign born in U. S., 70.

Economic gain by immigration, chapter VI, 93-122.
—— causes of emigration, 31; of immigration, 44.
—— effects of Chinese immigration, 244.
—— problems, character of, 2.
—— prosperity, effect of, on immigrants, 73.
—— value of the immigrant, 104-111.
—— well-being, in America, 6; effect of immigration on, 8.
Emigrants, age and sex of, 28; money taken with, 98; economic value of, 110; occupations of, 114; protecting the, 201; treatment of, on board ship, 215. See Emigration.
Emigration, history of, chapter II, 12-32; a phenomenon of modern life, 12, 15; statistics of, 15; from Great Britain, 17; from Germany, 18; other countries, 18; for years 1887 and 1888, 19; effect of, on population, 21-26; effect of voluntary emigration, 27; opposed by European governments, 27; causes of, 30; no longer going among strangers, 49; economic loss by, 111; assisted emigration, chapter IX, 168-200; from Switzerland, 170-171; assisted, by British government, 173-176; by Tuke Committee, 176-180; Association for State-directed Emigration, 180-185; prepaid tickets, 186-193; colonies assist, 193-195; Emigrants' Information Office, 196, 199; artificial stimulus to, 196; regulation

of, 205-214; right of, chapter XIII, 284-302.
England, emigration from, 19; per 1000 inhabitants, 21; excess of births over deaths, 23; importation of Flemish weavers, 35; immigration into U. S. from, since 1820, 67; born in, 69; paupers returned to, 160. See also Great Britain.
English language, influence of, 74.
Ethnical composition of population of U. S., 62.
Expatriation, declared to be a natural and inherent right, 228; anarchical in principle, 299.
Extra-territorial consular jurisdiction in China, 230.

Farmers and farm laborers among immigrants, 115.
Foreigners, descendants of, in U. S., 58; French decree in respect to, 270.
Foreign born, in U. S., 1880, 68; distribution of, 70; in cities, 71; intermarriage among, 76; voting population among, 80; influence of vote, 86; leaders of socialism, 88; in occupations in U. S., 94-96, 125; proportion among insane, 153-155; among defective classes, 150-153, 155-157; among prisoners and convicts, 157; among paupers, 158-161; among illiterates, 161-165.
Foreign parentage, persons of, in U. S., 58, 68; in cities of Massachusetts, 71; influence of American life on persons of, 73-76; of prisoners and convicts, 158; of paupers and homeless children, 159; of illiterates, 164.
France (and French), emigration from, 19; per 1000 inhabitants, 21; immigration to U. S. since 1820, 67; born in, 69; paupers returned to, 160; decree in respect to foreigners residing in, 270; contracts on public works in, excluding foreign workmen, 271 n.

French Canadians, naturalization of, 80; in cotton-mills of New England, 127, 130; character of, 135; influence of, in New England, 144; illiteracy among, 162-164; social influence of, 166.
French philosophy, influence of, 228, 288.
—— revolution, epoch of, 1, 285, 287-295.

Germany (and Germans), emigration from, 16, 18; per 1000 inhabitants, 21-22; excess of births over deaths, 23; evasion of military service, 27, 202; effect of emigration on population, 29; age of emigrants, 28; emigration from Alsace-Lorraine, 31; famine in 1853, 44; steamship fares from, 47; emigration of families, 50; children among, 51; immigrants to U. S. since 1820, 67; proportion to other nationalities, 67; persons of German parentage, 68; born in, 69; distribution of, in U. S., 70; in cities, 71; attachment to fatherland, 73; language, 75; intermarriage with other nationalities, 76; vote of, 86; in productive occupations in U. S., 96; money brought by emigrants, 99; *per capita* wealth in, 101; cost of rearing children, 104; capitalized value of emigrants, 111; occupations of emigrants, 114; paupers returned to, 160; illiteracy among, 162; convicts from, 172; emigration law, 209; expulsion of Slavic population, 270; conventions in regard to German paupers, 273; treatment of stranger in middle ages, 285.
Great Britain (and British), emigration from, 16-19; per 1000 inhabitants, 21; persons of British parentage, 68; in productive occupations in U. S., 96; money sent back to, 100; capitalized value of emigrants from, 110; occupations

of emigrants, 114; government assistance to emigration, 173-176; Emigrants' Information Office, 196; passengers' acts, 205, 208; British colonies and Chinese, 263-265. See also England, Ireland and Scotland.

Head-tax, on immigrants, imposed by state of New York, 221; declared unconstitutional, 223; imposed by Congress, 224; by California on Chinese, 238.

Holland, emigration from, 19; paupers returned to, 160.

Homeless children, in Massachusetts, 158.

Humanity, demands of, 301.

Hungary (and Hungarians), emigration from, 19; small number of females among, 50; in mines, 127; imported laborers, 131 n.; standard of living of, 134; social influence of, 166. See also Austria-Hungary.

Idiots, among foreign born in Massachusetts, 156.

Illiteracy, in U. S., 161; in Massachusetts, 162-165.

Immigrants, age, sex and occupation of, 50; distinction between, and colonists, 35; descendants of, in U. S., 58; destination of, 69; money brought by, 97-102; economic value of, 102-111; age of, 103; do we need the? 113; occupations of, 114; number of laborers among, 115; in factories, 125-126; displace American laborers, 127; under contract, 129; low standard of living, 131; treatment of, 219; Castle Garden, 221; head-tax on, 223; right to expel pauper, 268-270; number of, returned under act of 1882, 275.

Immigration, character of the question of, 4; very complex problem, 9; method of solution, 10; history of, chapter III, 33-52; importance of, 33; into U. S., 35-43; statistics of, 40; causes of, 43; effect of, on population, chapter IV, 53-78; represents an increase of births, 61; effect on ethnical composition of population, 62, 65; political effects of, chapter V, 79-92; economic gain by, chapter VI, 93-122; competition with American labor, chapter VII, 123-146; of skilled labor, 125; and a protective tariff, 128; social effects of, chapter VIII, 147-167; assisted, 193-195; Chinese, chapter XI, 227-265; restrictions on, chapter XII, 266-283; methods of restricting, 278-283; right of, chapter XIII, 284-302.

Immobility of labor, 139.

Increase, natural, in U. S., 60.

Indemnity, payment of, to Chinese, 259.

Industry, expansion of, 287.

Insanity among foreign born, 153.

International law, principles of, in regard to migration, 297.

Ireland (and Irish), emigration from, 19 n.; per 1000 of population, 21-22; excess of births over deaths, 23; effect of emigration on population, 24; famine in, 44; sex of immigrants, 50; age of immigrants, 51; immigrants since 1820, 67; relative number of, 67; Irish parentage, 68; born in, 69; distribution of, 70; in cities, 71; intermarriage with other nationalities, 76; naturalization of, 80; Irish vote, 86; in productive occupations in U. S., 96; paupers in Massachusetts, 159 n.; paupers returned to, 160; illiteracy among, 163; assisted emigration from, 173, 174, 177.

Italy (and Italians), emigration from, 19; per 1000 inhabitants, 21; sex of immigrants, 50; immigrants since 1820, 67; relative number, 67; in cities, 71; naturalization of, 80;

money sent back, 101; age of emigrants, 115; contract labor, 129-131; social condition of, 132-134; paupers returned to, 160; illiteracy among, 162, 164; induced immigration, 191-193; emigration law, 210; residence of aliens in, 269.

Know-Nothing party in U. S., 81; spirit of, 278.

Labor, foreign born, in U.S., 94; need of, in former times, 97; gained by the U. S., 102; unskilled, among immigrants, 115; unskilled always most abundant, 118; no need of further, 121; competition with American labor, chapter VII, 123-146; displacement of, 127; in the British colonies, 199 n.; competition of Chinese, 245-247. See Contract Labor.
Labor-force, original, in U. S., 54.
Laborers, benefited by competition, 142; exclusion of Chinese, 255, 260, 262.
Land, supply of, in U. S., 56; simplified social problem, 56.
Laws regulating emigration, 209-214.
Legislation, of U. S. in regard to immigration, 273-277; should be enforced, 279-281; against Chinese, 251, 255, 257, 261, 262; of California against Chinese, 238, 240; of France in respect to foreigners, 270; extension of, in regard to immigration, 297.
Letters to friends, 48.
Loss by emigration, 111.

Manufacturing industries of U. S., foreign born in, 95.
Marriage of different nationalities with each other, 75.
Massachusetts, foreign born in, 71; voting population, 80; persons of foreign parentage in cities, 71; defective classes, 156; prisoners and convicts, 157; paupers and homeless children, 158; illiteracy in, 162-165; unemployed in, 121.
Mechanical and mining industries, foreign born in, 95.
Mediæval restrictions on emigration, 285.
Migration, inherent right of, 228; right of, 284, 288, 290, 296.
Military service, evasion of, 27; restricts emigration, 202.
Miners' license tax, in California, 239.
Mixed races, theory of, 77.
Money brought by immigrants, 97, 98; sent back, 99, 101.
Municipal government, effect of immigration on, 87.
Murders of Chinese, 257.

National Association for State-directed Emigration, 180-184.
Nationality, of immigrants, 67; of foreign born, 68; of persons of foreign parentage, 68; in states, 70; in cities, 71; in naturalization, 80; in occupations, 96.
Natives, descendants of, in U. S., 59.
Native born, voters, 80; paupers, 158; illiterates, 162.
Native parentage, prisoners and convicts of, 158; paupers and homeless children, 159; illiterates, 164.
Natural right, of migration, 228, 284; doctrine of, 228, 290.
Naturalization, of different nationalities, 80; law of U. S., 82; policy of, 84; recent court decisions, 85; of Chinese, 235.
Negroes, in U. S., 64.
Nervous diseases, tendency of foreign born to, 155.
New England, French Canadians in, 135, 144.
New York, foreign born in, 70; Italians in city, 132; insanity among foreign born in, 154; pauperism in, 158; pauper aliens removed by State Board of Charities, 159; legislation to protect immigrants,

220; Commissioners of emigration, 220, 222, 225.

Norway, emigration from, 18, 19; per 1000 inhabitants, 21; since 1820, 67; born in, 69; paupers returned to, 160. See Scandinavians.

Occupations, of immigrants, 51, 72, 113, 125; of emigrants from Great Britain, 114; from Germany, 114; from Italy, 115; unskilled, 117; foreign born in, 94–96.

Over-population, emigration as a remedy for, 24, 25.

Parentage, persons of foreign, 68; of prisoners and convicts in Massachusetts, 158; of paupers and homeless children, 159; of illiterates, 164.

Passengers' acts, British, 205–208; U. S., 216.

Patriotism, foundation of, 5.

Paupers, assisted to emigrate, 169; by Swiss cantons, 170; by British government, 173; by Tuke Committee, 176; by charitable societies, 185; removed by New York State Board of Charities, 160; by U. S., 275; expulsion of, by Belgium, 272; of foreign birth or parentage, 158, 159.

Poles, character of immigrants, 132.

Political institutions, in America, 4; effect of immigration on, 6, chapter V, 79–92.

—— rights, exercise of, 73.

—— problems, in history, 1.

Population, effect of emigration on, 21, 23; in U. S. during colonial period, 37; from 1783 to 1820, 39; effect of immigration on, chapter IV, 53–78; growth of, in U. S., 53; of U. S. in 1790, 54; causes of growth of, 56; proportion due to immigrants, 58; ethnical composition of, in U. S., 62; elements of, in U. S., 64; negroes in, 64;

foreign element in, 67; parentage of, 68; birth-place of, 68; fusion of, 72; intermarriage of, 75; of voting age, 80.

Portuguese, naturalization of, 80; illiteracy, 162.

Prisoners and convicts of foreign birth or parentage, 157.

Proletariat, Marx's theory of an industrial, 121.

Protecting the emigrant, chapter X, 201–226.

Protective tariff and free immigration, 128.

Protest of U. S. against assisted emigration, 175.

Prussia, emigration from, per 1000 inhabitants, 22, 23, 25.

Railroads, effect of, in settling U. S., 57.

Remittances by immigrants to friends, 99, 101, 187.

Restriction on emigration, 202, 210, 212; mediæval, 285; right to restrict, 296.

—— on immigration, chapter XII, 266–283; right to restrict, 296–302.

Right of migration, 228, 229, 269, 284, 290.

Right to control emigration and immigration, chapter XIII, 284–302.

Rock Springs riots, 257.

Russia, emigration from, 20; contract-labor, 131 n.; paupers returned to, 160.

Scandinavian, persons of, parentage, 68; in Northwest, 146.

Scotland, emigration from, 19; per 1000 inhabitants, 21; since 1820, 67; born in, 69; paupers returned to, 160.

Social effects of immigration, chapter VIII, 147–167.

—— science, complexity of, 8.

Social traits, in America, effect of immigration on, 7, 166.

—— —— of Chinese, 242.

Index. 315

Socialism, in U. S., 88, 91.
Societies, charitable, assist emigration, 172, 176, 185.
Sex, proportion of, among immigrants, 28.
Skilled laborers among immigrants, 125.
Southern Immigration Society, 195.
Sovereignty of a nation over its own territory, 300.
Spain, emigration from, 20.
Standard of living, immigrants with low, 131.
State, end and purpose of the, 3; duty of, 292.
State-directed emigration, National association for, 180; destined to fail of its purpose, 195, 199.
Statistics, of emigration, 15; from Great Britain, 17; from Germany, 18; other countries, 19; of emigration per 1000 inhabitants, 21; of excess of births over deaths, 23; of immigration into U. S., 40; of insane, 153; of defective classes, 155; of criminals, 157; of pauperism, 158; of illiteracy, 161-165; of Chinese immigration, 236.
Steamships, sailing to New York, 46; agents, 46, 186; prepaid tickets, 188.
Sweating system, in New York and London, 136.
Sweden (and Swedes), emigration from, 18, 19; per 1000 inhabitants, 21; since 1820, 67; born in, 69; contract labor, 131 n.; paupers returned to, 160; illiteracy, 162; assisted emigrants, 185. See also Scandinavians.
Switzerland, emigration from, 20; per 1000 inhabitants, 21; since 1820, 67; paupers returned to, 160; emigration forbidden, 168; assisted emigration, 170, 171; law regulating emigration, 210-213.

Transportation, improved means of, 45-47, 186, 205, 216.

Treaties with China, 1844, 229; 1858, 230; 1868, 231; 1880, 253; abortive, 1888, 259.
Tuke Committee, 176.

Unemployed in U. S., 121; in Massachusetts, 121.
United States, The, statistics of immigration into, 16; history of immigration into, 35-52; population in, during colonial period, 37; population in, from 1783-1820, 39; immigration into, since 1820, 40; causes of immigration to, 43; growth of population in, 53; population in, 1790, 54; growth of settled area, 56; railroads, 57; effect of immigration on population of, 57, 61; proportion of natives and foreigners in, 58; effect of immigration on ethnical composition of population in, 62; nationalities in, 67; foreign born in, 68; foreign parentage in, 68; foreign born voters in, 80, 86; Know-Nothing party in, 81; naturalization law, 82-85; municipal government in, 87; outbreaks of anarchism and socialism, 88; economic gain by immigration, 94 ff.; occupations in, 94-96; money brought by immigrants to, 97; *per capita* wealth in, 101; labor brought to, 102; cost of bringing up children in, 105, 106; occupations of immigrants to, 113; need for unskilled labor in, 117; the unemployed in, 121; immigration of skilled labor, 125; foreign born in occupations, 126; contract laborers in, 129; Italians in, 133; sweating system in, 136; French Canadians and Scandinavians in, 144; mortality statistics of, 153; insanity in, 153; crime in, 157; pauperism, 158; illiteracy, 161; protest against assisted emigration, 175; Passengers' acts, 216; Chinese immigration, chapter XI, 227-265; law of 1882 restricting immigration, 273,

274, 280; law against contract labor, 276, 281.
Unskilled labor, 117; not in right place, 119.
Unrestricted immigration defended on economic grounds, 93; on humanitarian grounds, 288.

Value, economic, of the immigrant, 104–111; of the immigrant to us, 113.
Vote, foreign, influence of, 86.

Voting population in Massachusetts, 80.

Wages, capitalized value of, 110, 113; in sweating system, 137; effect of immigration on, 139.
Wealth per capita in Germany and United States, 101.
Well-being, average, decreased by immigration, 101.
Western states, foreign born in, 94, 95.

www.ingramcontent.com/pod-product-compliance
Lightning Source LLC
Chambersburg PA
CBHW030733230426
43667CB00007B/693